CW01617701

Seven Ways to Ignite Your Life

Seven Ways to Ignite Your Life

LIFE LESSONS FROM 1 SAMUEL

NIGEL JAMES

Authentic

ignite

12 11 10 09 08 07 06 7 6 5 4 3 2 1

First published 2006 by Authentic Media
9 Holdom Avenue, Bletchley, Milton Keynes, Bucks, MK1 1QR, UK
and 129 Mobilization Drive, Waynesboro, GA 30830-4575, USA
www.authenticmedia.co.uk

Authentic Media is a division of Send the Light Ltd., a company limited by guarantee (registered charity no. 270162)

British Library Cataloguing in Publication Data
A catalogue record for this book is available from the British Library

ISBN-13 978-1-85078-691-7
ISBN-10 1-85078-691-7

Print Management by Adare Carwin
Printed in Great Britain by J.H. Haynes & Co., Sparkford

CONTENTS

INTRODUCTION

Samuel and David. Two great Old Testament characters whose lives cross in the book of the Bible we call 1 Samuel. Most of the action in this book takes place around the time of 1000 BC when Saul was king. That's about midway between the time when God calls Abraham and the time when Jesus was born.

David was called a man after God's own heart, and Samuel's name literally meant 'Name of God', yet neither of them was by any means perfect. Examining their lives doesn't give us two unattainable examples of spiritual superstars, but does provide guidance about how ordinary people can become extraordinary when they are determined to live lives that glorify God.

There's loads of great stories, action and adventure in 1 Samuel. We won't be covering all of it in this book. Instead we'll be focusing on seven incidents from either the life of Samuel or David, and in a couple of instances both.

The seven incidents clearly give us wisdom and direction for our own everyday living. If we can take these life lessons on board, then our journey with Jesus will be ignited with a dramatic new intensity and our lives will become much more fruitful.

We start with God calling out to Samuel in the dead of night; we move onto the Ark returning to Israel, and then we learn about David's friendship with Jonathan. We will also be examining the turning point in Israel's history when Samuel points out Saul's disobedience, and as a result identifies David as the future king. Finally we investigate two of David's great victories – one as a young man over Goliath, and one as a mighty warrior over the Amalekites.

So often I've struggled to make the transition from biblical truth to everyday life, and you might well be the same. Writing this book has helped me personally bridge that gap, and my prayer is that it will do the same for you.

In each chapter of this book, as well as the main unpacking of the Bible story, you'll find some other things to help you. The 'key verse' will get you right to the heart of the issue and can be used as a memory verse if you like. 'Reasons I don't Ignite' will demonstrate to you some of the symptoms that can lead us to having a less than passionate relationship with God and can be used as warning signals in our own lives. 'Honesty moments' will help you take a minute or two to reflect upon what you've been reading and will help you make an appropriate response.

Each chapter also has plenty of stories and illustrations for you to enjoy, and a few times I've asked a great friend of mine called Andy Booth to help us out by giving his insight into the theme of the chapter.

The chapters of this book started out as devotional talks for our very first Ignite UK tour back in 2001, so in part I want to dedicate the book to everyone who has ever worked with Big Ideas and Ignite – especially Gary Smith and Anita Monks who have been part of the scene since the very beginning.

I also used the themes in the book as a series of devotions with the band Third Day for one of the US tours on which I accompanied them. This book is dedicated to the guys in Third Day too: Mac, David, Tai, Mark, Brad, and my good friend on the road, Geof. Thanks also to Andy Booth for adding some insights to three of the chapters, and to his wife Trish for letting Andy spend so much time with me when I'm in Fort Wayne.

Finally I want to thank my family, especially my wife Gill and daughter Bethan, for allowing me to escape regularly to our caravan on the Gower peninsula so that I could write this book.

Nigel James
Gower, October 2005

1 LISTEN TO THE VOICE OF GOD

It's the time of Hannukah in Jerusalem – a Jewish festival of Dedication, and the crowds are pouring into the area known as Solomon's Colonnade. The celebrations are different this year because Jesus has turned up, and the assembled gathering soon turns nasty. Not for the first time they begin to pick up the biggest rocks they can lay their hands on, ready to chuck them at Jesus. Why? Good question. The crowd had been begging Jesus to let them know if he was the Messiah or not, and Jesus had simply been walking around, minding his own business.

In response to the pleading of the crowd he talks about his Father, about sheep and about eternal life, and suddenly the crowd are shouting 'blasphemy' because Jesus has had the cheek to say, 'I and the Father are one.' John describes this scene for us in the tenth chapter of his Gospel, and in the middle of Jesus' words to the crowd he says this incredible statement: 'My sheep listen to my voice; I know them, and they follow me.' (Jn. 10:27, NIV)

The Jews swarming around Jesus are so outraged at his claims to be one with God that they don't take much notice of this little sentence. Jesus is saying that he is the shepherd and that his followers, the sheep, are looked after by him. He states that sheep can listen to and follow the voice of the shepherd.

What an amazing thought. Can we really listen to the voice of God? Does God really speak? Does he know us so well that he can speak to each of us as individuals? Well, if Jesus said it then it must be true, and we are going to start our journey in Samuel 1 by tackling some of those questions.

God calls out to Samuel

The nation of Israel was being led by a series of leaders called Judges, and more often than not it had been a bit of a disaster. In the not too distant future, Samson would bring the time of the Judges to an embarrassing end.

The country needed a leader to believe in; one who could be trusted. Hannah was a woman who had been unable to have children, and so she struck a bargain with God. It went something like this: she promised that if God gave her a son then she'd make sure the boy was dedicated to serving God all his life. So that's what happened. Hannah literally gave her son back to God by placing the young Samuel into the care of Eli the high priest.

There was just one problem. Eli had sons of his own, and they were a big embarrassment. They kept on messing up big time, and Eli did nothing to sort them out. The sons were described as wicked – that's old fashioned wicked, not 'cool' style wicked! Stealing some of the offerings and sleeping with the women-servants at the Tent of Meeting were just a couple of things that Eli's boys got up to.

That's the scene when we come to the night that God calls out to Samuel:

Meanwhile, the boy Samuel was serving the LORD by assisting Eli. Now in those days messages from the LORD were very rare, and visions were quite uncommon.

One night Eli, who was almost blind by now, had just gone to bed. The lamp of God had not yet gone out, and Samuel was sleeping in the Tabernacle near the Ark of God. Suddenly, the LORD called out, 'Samuel!'

'Yes?' Samuel replied. 'What is it?' He got up and ran to Eli. 'Here I am. Did you call me?'

'I didn't call you,' Eli replied. 'Go on back to bed.' So he did.

Then the LORD called out again, 'Samuel!'

Again Samuel jumped up and ran to Eli. 'Here I am. Did you call me?'

'I didn't call you, my son,' Eli said. 'Go on back to bed.'

Samuel did not yet know the LORD because he had never had a message from the LORD before. So now the LORD called a third time, and once more Samuel got up and went to Eli. 'Here I am. Did you call me?'

Then Eli realized it was the LORD who was calling the boy. So he said to Samuel, 'Go and lie down again, and if someone calls again, say, "Speak, LORD, your servant is listening."' So Samuel went back to bed.

And the LORD came and called as before, 'Samuel! Samuel!'

And Samuel replied, 'Speak, your servant is listening.' (1 Sam. 3:1-10)

From the story above we discover that messages and visions from God were rare. That's actually a bit of an understatement because in the whole period of the Judges – about 300 years or so – there were only two prophets and five revelations. Yet in this encounter, God calls out to Samuel in a way that he hadn't done for centuries.

At this time Samuel was probably about twelve years of age, and was acting as the eyes for the old priest Eli who had failing sight. In the middle of the night though, it wasn't his eyes that were worrying Samuel; instead he must have begun to think that his ears were playing tricks on him. Even more astounding, we are told that 'Samuel did not yet know the LORD.' In other words, Samuel had no direct experience of God because he hadn't encountered God personally.

Can you put yourself in this scene? You are just dozing off and a voice wakes you up. Are you scared? Confused? Annoyed? Inquisitive? Or do you just roll over, put the pillow over your head and go back to your dreams? Hold on a minute, perhaps the voice is a dream in the first place?

My best friend at university was a guy called Kevan Eveleigh, and one night I decided to hide myself in the wardrobe of his bedroom in our Hall of Residence. Don't ask me why, but it seemed a good idea at the time. When Kev came in and went to bed I began to 'meeow' softly like a cat.

He got up out of bed, wandered around the room looking for a stray moggy, gave up and went back to bed without finding me. My attempts at scratching sounds brought the same results, so eventually I began to gently call out his name in a high-pitched whine.

Kev was really confused; he checked the radio, looked outside the window, opened the door and peered down the corridor. Eventually he pulled open the wardrobe to discover me sitting there! He hadn't been expecting anyone to be calling out his name just as he was dozing off to sleep – let alone someone sitting in his wardrobe!

KEY VERSE

And the LORD came and called as before, 'Samuel! Samuel!' And Samuel replied, 'Speak, your servant is listening.' (1 Sam. 3:10)

God's voice

Three times God calls out to Samuel, and three times Samuel thinks he's being called by Eli the priest. Each time, eager to please, Samuel responds to the voice and goes over to Eli. It isn't until the third time that Eli realizes exactly what's going on. Eli suggests that when God calls again, Samuel should respond with these words: 'Speak, your servant is listening.'

The story of God calling Samuel teaches us a few important lessons for life:

- God calls people by name
- You can mistake God's voice for a human one

- Sometimes you need another person to tell you that it's God speaking
- A bit of peace and quiet really helps when listening to God

Let's examine these one at a time.

God calls you by name

When God called Samuel he used his name. Kind of obvious isn't it, but some people believe God isn't interested in each of us personally. He just shouts out some random stuff and if you hear it… lucky you. The truth is that God was calling Samuel for a purpose, and the fact that God knew his name indicated that God knew everything about him and was interested in Samuel as a person.

The Bible is full of people God called by name. Here are two Old Testament examples, one from before the time of Samuel and one from after, showing how the Lord God calls people by name to follow him:

> *When the LORD saw that he had caught Moses' attention, God called to him from the bush, 'Moses! Moses!'*
>
> *'Here I am!' Moses replied. (Ex. 3:4)*
>
> *Then the LORD said to me, 'Look, Jeremiah! What do you see?' (Jer. 1:11)*

By the time we get into the New Testament, the Lord Jesus goes into overdrive as he calls people by name:

> *But the Lord said to her, 'My dear Martha.' (Lk. 10:41)*
>
> *'Mary!' Jesus said. She turned toward him and exclaimed, 'Teacher!' (Jn. 20:16)*

When Jesus came by, he looked up at Zacchaeus and called him by name. 'Zacchaeus!' he said. 'Quick, come down! For I must be a guest in your home today.' (Lk. 19:5)

Jesus replied, 'You are blessed, Simon son of John, because my Father in heaven has revealed this to you.' (Mt. 16:17)

Then Jesus shouted, 'Lazarus, come out!'(Jn. 11:43)

He fell to the ground and heard a voice saying to him, 'Saul! Saul! Why are you persecuting me?' (Acts 9:4)

Now there was a believer in Damascus named Ananias. The Lord spoke to him in a vision, calling, 'Ananias!'

'Yes, Lord!' he replied. (Acts 9:10)

You can see that the Lord God knows all his people by name, and even calls some pretty unlikely people by name. Imagine the stunned look on the face of the small-time crook Zacchaeus when Jesus gives him the call to come on down!

Names had special significance in biblical times. Children were given names that meant something; names carried status and people became known and valued because of the significance of their name. In some instances they were re-named or given a nickname in order to serve a specific purpose.

If nobody knew your name then you were really insignificant – a bit like the extras at the bottom of a long list of actors in a hit movie. They only play a really small part, and the role they play isn't even important enough to be given a name. They are just 'fifth policeman' or 'face in the crowd'.

I have to admit that I'm terrible with names. I can be introduced to someone one minute and have forgotten the person's name the next. I often have to say quietly to a friend, 'Who was that person I was just talking to?' That's terrible isn't it!

You know how humiliating it can be when someone doesn't know your name or forgets it. You feel worthless and want the ground to swallow you up. The call of Samuel wouldn't really have worked if God had said, 'Oi mate, whatever your name is! Hey there thingy, yeah you. I want a word.'

God isn't like that! He wasn't like that with Samuel and he isn't like that with you. You are famous; the God who created the heavens and the earth knows your name and calls you by it.

There is a warning however. Someone asks Jesus if everyone will have eternal life and be part of God's family forever. This is his answer: 'The door to heaven is narrow. Work hard to get in, because many will try to enter, but when the head of the house has locked the door, it will be too late. Then you will stand outside knocking and pleading, "Lord, open the door for us!" But he will reply, "I do not know you." (Lk. 13:24-25)

When you approach the heavenly gates, you can go forward with complete confidence if you have put your trust and faith in Jesus. For those who haven't done so, that will be the time that the Lord Jesus doesn't call by name. They will hear this phrase ringing in their ears, 'I do not know you.'

You can mistake God's voice for a human one

We've already heard that Samuel mistook the voice of God for the voice of Eli and repeated this mistake three times. It's an easy mistake to make. I can remember the first real encounter I had with God. It happened in my bedroom as a teenager; in an instant late one night I knew that God was calling me to serve him. There was no audible voice or angelic appearance, but I knew God had spoken to me.

After a few weeks though, doubt set in. Had it really been God? Was I speaking to myself? Had I just taken on board the suggestions of other people? Thankfully, God has confirmed that call time and again.

Sometimes we can hear God's voice and not recognize it because we don't believe he'd speak to us personally. Other times we might hear God speak to us through another person and still not really hear God. Then again, we might mistake the honest encouragement or suggestions of other people for the voice of God.

Keep tuned in!

The story is told of a man who bought a new radio. He immediately tuned it into his favourite station and then broke the tuning dial off so that it could never be tuned into anything else!

In the busy-ness and noise of life, do you think there are times when you have tuned out to God and tuned into other things? One of my own biggest challenges is to tune out the selfish voice that comes from deep inside me. How could you stay tuned into God? There is some advice at the end of this chapter called 'Listening to God' that you might find helpful.

Honesty time

Have an honesty moment with God right now. If God were to call you by name, what else would you like him to say? Imagine a sentence from God beginning with your name. Deep down in your heart, what would that sentence be?

Sometimes you need someone else to tell you that God is speaking

Samuel needed the older and more experienced Eli to help him recognize the voice of God. More than that, Eli even pointed out to Samuel the way to respond. His guidance to Samuel is perfect guidance for us today when we are waiting to hear the voice of God: 'Speak, your servant is listening.'

If you are not confident that God is speaking to you or you aren't sure what he's saying, then seek the help of a Christian friend. Asking them to tell you if they believe that God is speaking to you, and what they think God might be saying, will be a real help.

Peace and quiet help when listening to God

It's important to note that God spoke to Samuel when he was asleep. God still speaks to people in their sleep – just wander into any church service and you'll see what I mean. Only joking!

Often God will use dreams and visions to speak to his people, and these may well come in the night. The most important thing, however, is to realize that you will miss hearing the voice of God if you are too busy and too preoccupied, listening to a million and one other distractions. Samuel was calm and resting when God spoke to him.

First of all Samuel didn't realize it was God, but he was ready to answer and ready to make himself available. He ended up in a servant relationship with God in a way that Eli's sons never did. Samuel became so captivated and excited by the Word of God that eventually his own words and God's word became virtually the same thing.

REASONS I DON'T IGNITE

1. Insecurity

Insecurity can do real damage to our passion for Jesus. If we feel insecure and unworthy in our relationship with God then we begin to believe he wouldn't want to speak to us, and we don't listen out for his voice. The Apostle Paul had no illusions about the type of person he used to be, but realized it was exactly because he was unworthy and sinful that God did want to speak to him and give him eternal security:

This is a true saying, and everyone should believe it. Christ Jesus came into the world to save sinners – and I was the worst of them all. But that is why God had mercy on me, so that Christ Jesus could use me as a prime example of his great patience with even the worst sinners. Then others will realize that they, too, can believe in him and receive eternal life. (1 Tim. 1:15-16)

Jesus called Saul by name and spoke to him. Because of his past he deserved to be insecure before God, but instead Jesus changed his name to Paul and used him mightily.

God created you, wants you back, wants to forgive you and wants you to have eternal security. God knows your name – how much more secure do you need to be?

'I took you from the ends of the earth, from its farthest corners I called you. I said, "You are my servant"; I have chosen you and have not rejected you.' (Is. 41:9, NIV)

So here's where the rubber hits the road. How do we get practical and learn to listen to the voice of God? I've asked my good friend Andy Booth, who is a ministry coach at Heartland Community Church in Fort Wayne, Indiana, to give us some helpful suggestions.

LISTENING TO GOD

'My sheep listen to my voice; I know them, and they follow me.' (Jn. 10:27, NIV)

When you begin listening to God you'll be able to say:

- I'll get to know Jesus better.
- He'll know more about me. (There aren't any secrets, but everything will be out in the open.)
- I'll start to reflect God's character.
- I'll learn to be responsible for feeding myself spiritually.
- My deepest needs will be met.
- I'll find a secure place.

THE PLACE

You need to find a place to listen to God. It might well be a real, physical place, but it needs to be a spiritual place inside you too.

Be still, and know that I am God; I will be exalted among the nations, I will be exalted in the earth. (Ps. 46:10, NIV)

A place of relaxation is a place of revelation, so learn to be still and quiet before God. Learn to get close to him and to enjoy intimacy. Find somewhere away from distractions and noise.

'Quiet, everyone! Shh! Silence before God. Something's afoot in his holy house. He's on the move!' (Zech. 2:13, *The Message*)

This place will be:

1. A PLACE TO DISCOVER IDENTITY

Let God speak to you and tell you who you really are. God will show you that you are his son, one of his flock, a royal subject, a precious child... and so much more. Imagine God speaking out loud to you and calling you by name. What would he say? What other encouraging names from the Bible would he call you?

'For all who are led by the Spirit of God are children of God.' (Rom. 8:14)

2. A PLACE TO DISCOVER PROTECTION

Get used to discovering God's peace and security when you listen to his voice.

'So let us come boldly to the throne of our gracious God. There we will receive his mercy, and we will find grace to help us when we need it.' (Heb. 4:16)

The word for help that the writer to the Hebrews uses is the same word used in Acts 27 that describes the ropes that hold a ship together in a storm. God can calm the storm and he can hold us together in the storm. Allow God to speak to you when you need protection so that you can hear his voice of comfort.

3. A PLACE TO DISCOVER PROVISION

When you begin to hear God's voice in the stillness you will begin to lose burdens and worries. Ask God to take away your hurts and your concerns, get ready to see him provide for you.

'Don't worry about anything; instead, pray about everything. Tell God what you need, and thank him for all he has done.' (Phil. 4:6)

Just like you'd go to the local supermarket to stock up on food, or you'd go to the cinema for the latest blockbuster, get used to going to God and letting him provide for you.

THE PRACTICALITIES

These are the jump leads – to connect an empty, dead battery to a full, live one.

- Expectancy/Attitude.
- A quiet place (no phone, radio, TV, computer).
- Schedule regular time to listen to God. (Fifteen minutes each morning? Fifteen minutes earlier to bed? Grow the time as you go on.)
- Find your entry point into stillness. Is it worship? Creativity?
- Balance. Try a combination of worship, study, prayer and silence. (One each day if you can't manage them all.)
- Listen closely.
- Write down what God says.

EXTRA HELPS

How about trying some of the following?

- The Bible on tape.
- Bible study notes.
- Email/Website devotions.
- A concordance.
- A journal.
- A different Bible translation.
- A comfortable body position (ever tried lying face down?).
- Praying the prayers that others have written – either in the Bible or in prayer books.

- Using the Psalms as prayers.
- Spending a longer time with God. A retreat or half-day.
- Worship CDs (occasionally make your quiet time with God a loud time!).

2 COMMIT YOURSELF TO THE WORSHIP OF GOD

The ball soars between the rugby goal posts and 70,000 screaming Welsh supporters go wild. Gavin Henson has kicked a penalty goal from miles away and Wales are about to beat England at rugby for the first time in ages. A whole nation rejoices, and Henson is transformed into a hero.

Worship? It comes naturally to us; it's just that these days it's mostly sportsmen and women or pop stars who receive our adulation. The issue isn't do we worship; the issue is who we worship.

Funnily enough, that's exactly the issue Samuel faced when we next meet him. He continued to be close to the Lord and as he listened to the voice of God he was able to act as God's spokesman around the nation of Israel:

> *'As Samuel grew up, the LORD was with him, and everything Samuel said was wise and helpful. All the people of Israel from one end of the land to the other knew that Samuel was confirmed as a prophet of the LORD.' (1 Sam. 3:19-20)*

Yet times were difficult. The Israelites were at war with the Philistines and the battles were going so badly that they decided to carry the Ark of the Covenant with them as they sought a victory. The Ark of the Covenant was a symbol of the presence and glory of God. It was considered holy and its resting place was considered sacred. The Ark had been carried around the walls of Jericho by Joshua and his troops in a great victory many years before, but now Eli the old man received some bad news:

The man who brought the news replied, 'Israel fled before the Philistines, and the army has suffered heavy losses. Also your two sons, Hophni and Phinehas, are dead, and the ark of God has been captured.'

When he mentioned the ark of God, Eli fell backward off his chair by the side of the gate. His neck was broken and he died, for he was an old man and heavy. He had led Israel for forty years.' (1 Sam. 4:17-18, NIV)

So Eli, the priest who had brought Samuel up was dead. Eli's daughter-in-law was pregnant, and the shock of the Ark's capture led to her dying in childbirth, but before she died:

She named the boy Ichabod, saying, 'The glory has departed from Israel' – because of the capture of the ark of God and the deaths of her father-in-law and her husband. She said, 'The glory has departed from Israel, for the ark of God has been captured.' (1 Sam. 4:21-22, NIV)

Israel's greatest treasure and the representation of its unique relationship with the Lord had been stolen and taken away by the Philistines. They only actually kept hold of it for seven months, but in that time they suffered a series of disasters. They put the Ark of the Covenant next to their own Philistine idols and twice their idols fell over and were damaged. The people of the city of Ashdod where the Ark was being held began to get a plague of tumours, and when they moved the Ark to the city of Gath, the same happened to their inhabitants.

Eventually the Philistines decided to send the Ark back to Israel because it had been so unlucky for them. They even sent guilt offerings back with it. It was returned first of all to a town called Beth Shemesh, but seventy local men died because they looked into the Ark and couldn't survive the glory of God. In the end some men from Kiriath Jearim collected the Ark of the Covenant.

You would think that the Israelites would have been overjoyed at having the Ark back. The symbol of God's presence and glory was now with them again. Far from it! The people were so half-hearted about worshipping the Lord and giving him his rightful place that they left the Ark of the Covenant in the little town of Kiriath Jearim for twenty years. It took David, when he was king, to restore the Ark to pride of place when he built a special tent for it in Jerusalem.

During the time when the Ark was still in Kiriath Jearim, all of Israel was sad because they felt that the Lord had abandoned them. They were complaining about problems but refusing to act. They moaned that God had abandoned them but didn't stop to recognize that they had abandoned worshipping God. It's an incredible story really!

The nearest modern equivalent I can think of would be if the Crown Jewels had been stolen and then returned on a cross-channel ferry to Dover, and taken to a small country village. Instead of being returned to their rightful place in the Tower of London the jewels would sit in someone's house for twenty years!

Returning to the story, the Israelites in the meantime set up idols of foreign gods. They hoped that Baal would help them grow crops, and that Ashtoreth would help them and the land become fertile. The Israelites were sad that the Lord God had abandoned them but still didn't bother to give priority to the symbol of the Lord's glory and presence. Instead they worshipped false gods. It was Samuel who knew that action was required:

> *Then Samuel said to all the people of Israel, 'If you are really serious about wanting to return to the LORD, get rid of your foreign gods and your images of Ashtoreth. Determine to obey only the LORD; then he will rescue you from the Philistines.' So the Israelites got rid of their images of Baal and Ashtoreth and worshiped only the LORD.*

Then Samuel told them, 'Come to Mizpah, all of you. I will pray to the LORD for you.' So they gathered at Mizpah and, in a great ceremony, drew water from a well and poured it out before the LORD. They also went without food all day and confessed that they had sinned against the LORD. So it was at Mizpah that Samuel became Israel's judge. (1 Sam. 7:3-6)

Worship is sacrifice

Samuel recognized that it was no use pretending to worship the Lord when other foreign gods and images were being worshipped. He knew that God was jealous for the worship of the Israelites; this couldn't be shared by other gods. The NIV and King James Version translate this passage as 'returning to the LORD with all your hearts' and the NIV elsewhere translates it as 'commit yourselves to the LORD and serve him only.' Others such as *The Message* say 'worship him and him alone.'

In the passage above the reference to drawing water from a well and pouring it out before the Lord was an indication of repentance and humility. Samuel was beginning to lay the ground rules for what real worship was all about, and he kicked it off for the Israelites with a big prayer meeting that resulted in a victorious battle for the Israelites. Once again, Samuel was teaching the people a lesson – you can win a battle on your knees.

Samuel knew that true worship had to be an everyday sacrifice and not just an occasional, half-hearted, low-priority event. Samuel also knew that the Lord God was so mighty and so holy that he deserved total and complete worship; anything less would not give him the honour he deserved.

Deep down Samuel saw that worship was about sacrifice. It was here that Samuel became a Judge of Israel. That meant he was a political and religious ruler, and where most previous Judges relied on their own judgement, Samuel made sure he relied on God's judgement.

I've heard the following story told about so many famous preachers over the years I don't know which one it is actually truly about! The truth behind the story is powerful though. For the purposes of our story I'm going to call the famous preacher Bill Smith.

People travelled from far and wide to Bill Smiths' church in order to hear him preach. One Sunday he was taken ill and arranged for a friend to lead the service and preach in his place.

When it was announced that Bill Smith wouldn't be preaching, some people sighed with disappointment and walked out of the church. The replacement preacher stood up and said that those who had come to worship Bill Smith could leave, but those who had come to worship God would be welcome to stay.

It's very easy for all of us to replace 'God worship' with other forms of worship. How often do we turn up at church because we want to hear the speaker, or enjoy the worship leader's songs, or even just want to see our friends rather than to worship God?

KEY VERSE

Then Samuel said to all the people of Israel, 'If you are really serious about wanting to return to the LORD, get rid of your foreign gods and your images of Ashtoreth. Determine to obey only the LORD; then he will rescue you from the Philistines.' So the Israelites destroyed their images of Baal and Ashtoreth and worshipped only the LORD.
(1 Sam. 7:3-4)

Once, when David was king, the Lord instructed him to build an altar right on the site where a man called Araunah was threshing wheat. When Araunah heard that

David wanted to use his threshing floor for an altar, he was ready to give it to him for nothing and wanted to give the king oxen for a burnt offering, wheat for a grain offering, and tools to help build the altar. However, David had other ideas: 'David replied to Araunah, "No. I'm buying it from you, and at the full market price. I'm not going to offer GOD sacrifices that are no sacrifice." (1 Chr. 21:24, *The Message*)

In other words, David wasn't prepared to offer his worship to the Lord without it actually costing him something, without it actually being a proper sacrifice. One of the main tasks of the church is to worship God. That means attributing worth to him, giving him the honour that he is due.

In the twenty-first century we mostly think about worship as singing songs, and of course there are many biblical examples of offering praise to God in song. Yet worship is much more than singing: it's not a music style, it's a lifestyle. We worship not just with our lips but with our life.

WHAT DO WE SACRIFICE IN A LIFE OF WORSHIP?

If we should be everyday worshippers then what can we offer as sacrifice? How about some of these:

- Our minds

But if God himself has taken up residence in your life, you can hardly be thinking more of yourself than of him. Anyone, of course, who has not welcomed this invisible but clearly present God, the Spirit of Christ, won't know what we're talking about. (Rom. 8:9, The Message*)*

- Spend some time every day thinking about God – who he is, what he is like, and especially what he would think of a particular situation you are in. Is there an issue you are struggling with, or a decision you are about to make?

- Whenever you recognize yourself thinking bad, negative, ungodly thoughts, quickly ask God to help you change your way of thinking.

• Our bodies

And so, dear brothers and sisters, I plead with you to give your bodies to God. Let them be a living and holy sacrifice – the kind he will accept. When you think of what he has done for you, is this too much to ask? (Rom. 12:1)

- Remember that what you do with your body is an act of worship – so that means eating properly, getting rest and exercise, and not engaging in inappropriate physical acts.
- One of the Hebrew words for worship is *gahar*, which literally means laying down prostrate. You can worship God by actually laying your body down on the ground as a gesture of your humility and God's greatness. Try it in your prayer time.

• Our possessions and our money

Jesus felt genuine love for this man as he looked at him. 'You lack only one thing,' he told him. 'Go and sell all you have and give the money to the poor, and you will have treasure in heaven. Then come, follow me.'

At this, the man's face fell, and he went sadly away because he had many possessions. (Mk. 10:21-22)

- Remember that everything you own was given to you by God in the first place. Learn to be generous. Put a little money aside each day to go into the offering in church.
- Find out how to sponsor a child and commit to a regular amount of money each month to do so. The website www.compassionuk.org will help you do this.

- Our praise

With Jesus' help, let us continually offer our sacrifice of praise to God by proclaiming the glory of his name. (Heb. 13:15)

- Realize that worship is to an audience of one – God himself. Don't worry about people around you.
- Make space each day to offer God your praises. Remember the 'Listening to God' advice in chapter 1.
- There are three main Hebrew words for praise. Understanding them will help you:
  halal – making a noise.
  zamar – singing or playing instruments.
  yadah – bodily actions.

Honesty time

Have an honesty moment before God now. Are there any modern-day idols in your life that you need to get rid of so you can worship God?

Once Samuel had reached old age, he appointed his oldest sons Joel and Abijah to be Judges over Israel, but unfortunately they were both greedy and dishonest. The other leaders of Israel met and decided to ask Samuel to give them a king like all the other nations had. This request disappointed Samuel, and he reluctantly told the Lord about it:

> *'Do as they say to you,' the LORD replied, 'for it is me they are rejecting, not you. They don't want me to be their king any longer. Ever since I brought them from Egypt they have continually forsaken me and followed other gods. And now they are giving you the same treatment. Do as they ask, but solemnly warn them about how a king will treat them.' (1 Sam. 8:7-9)*

Samuel did as the Lord requested; he told the people that having a king would be a bad thing, and that it would signal a rebellion towards God. The people refused to listen and pleaded for a king. So the Lord led Samuel to choose Saul as king of Israel. Samuel anointed him and presented him to the Israelites. In a ceremony at Gilgal, Saul was crowned as king and Samuel, now old and grey, gave a farewell speech to the people of Israel.

He reminded them that he had served as their leader since being a boy, and that he had followed their wishes and given them a king – Saul – to lead them instead of any of Samuel's own sons. He talked of the numerous times they had turned away from the Lord by worshipping other images.

He even displayed God's power in action. It was the dry season, and Samuel asked God to send down thunder and rain to show the people how disobedient they had been to ask for a king. Sure enough, the Lord sent down thunder and rain and the people were terrified. Samuel had more to say:

'Don't be afraid,' Samuel reassured them. 'You have certainly done wrong, but make sure now that you worship the LORD with all your heart, and that you don't turn your back on him in any way. Don't go back to worshiping worthless idols that cannot help or rescue you – they really are useless! The LORD will not abandon his chosen people, for that would dishonor his great name. He made you a special nation for himself.

'As for me, I will certainly not sin against the LORD by ending my prayers for you. And I will continue to teach you what is good and right. But be sure to fear the LORD and sincerely worship him. Think of all the wonderful things he has done for you. But if you continue to sin, you and your king will be destroyed.' (1 Sam. 12:20-25)

So Samuel's final public words to the nation encouraged them to worship the Lord with all their hearts. It was the Lord who was really their king, and no-one else. Samuel challenged the people not to worship worthless idols – even human kings – and reminded them that the choice was theirs. They could worship the Lord or they could sin. It was up to them. Faithfulness, obedience and heartfelt worship are what really mark out the people of God.

REASONS I DON'T IGNITE

2. Illness

Worship is simply being preoccupied with God. If we suffer from spiritual illness, or what I call 'sin-sickness', then we will be so self-centred and pre-occupied with ourselves that we will never offer God the worship he deserves. Sin-sickness is the biggest enemy of worship; it pushes us into ourselves and our own little world rather than concentrating on God.

> *Focusing on the self is the opposite of focusing on God. Anyone completely absorbed in self ignores God, ends up thinking more about self than God. That person ignores who God is and what he is doing. (Rom. 8:7,* The Message*)*

Once we succumb to sin-sickness then everything else falls apart as well:

> *As long as you did what you felt like doing, ignoring God, you didn't have to bother with right thinking or right living, or right anything for that matter. (Rom. 6:20,* The Message*)*

Here's the good news! It's because we all suffer from sin-sickness that God sent his son into the world. It was to rescue us from this deadly illness that Jesus died on the cross.

It wasn't so long ago that we ourselves were stupid and stubborn, dupes of sin, ordered every which way by our glands, going around with a chip on our shoulder, hated and hating back. But when God, our kind and loving Savior God, stepped in, he saved us from all that. (Tit. 3:3-5, The Message*)*

When we recognize God's incredible love to us, poured out on the cross, isn't that worth all of our worship?

Born to be wild? No, born to worship!

Men and women were born to worship. Worship comes naturally to us. We can worship singers, TV celebrities, sports stars, boyfriends, girlfriends, the size of our bank account, the pursuit of power and success. We can even worship ourselves. Yet we weren't created to worship any of these people or things. We were created to worship the living God, and when we put that into practice we begin to be the children of God that we were meant to be.

People all around us are trying new ways of finding fulfilment by worshipping all types of strange things, but we know who placed the heart of worship inside us and we know who to worship for that heart to pump with real life and real love. Once again I've asked my good friend Andy Booth to give us his perspective on committing our daily lives to worship.

HOW WORSHIP CAN AFFECT THE REST OF OUR LIVES

Growing up, my favourite poster was of a surfer hooking a huge wave about to roll in. The phrase at the bottom said, 'Face your fears, live your dreams.' The more I reflected on that phrase, the more I realized that actually facing fears doesn't make them disappear or make living the dreams for life any easier. David discovered something about this in Psalm 27. Listen to what he says:

The Lord is my light and my salvation –
so why should I be afraid?
The Lord protects me from danger –
so why should I tremble?
When evil people come to destroy me,
when my enemies and foes attack me,
they will stumble and fall.
Though a mighty army surrounds me,
my heart will know no fear.
Even if they attack me,
I remain confident. (Ps. 27:1-3)

He sounds like someone who is living his dreams and has overcome his fears. So what is David's secret? The next two verses tell us:

The one thing I ask of the Lord,
the thing I seek most –
is to live in the house of the Lord all the days of my life,
delighting in the Lord's perfections
and meditating in his Temple.
For he will conceal me there when troubles come;

he will hide me in his sanctuary.
He will place me out of reach on a high rock.
(Ps. 27:3-4)

David had learned that the secret of overcoming fear was to focus on God in worship. As we learn to focus on God through worship our fears begin to subside and eventually disappear. The Bible talks a lot about this. Peter only got in trouble and experienced fearful walking on water when he removed his focus from Jesus.

In Isaiah 26:3 God has said, 'You will keep in perfect peace all who trust in you, whose thoughts are fixed on you!' We also see the same idea from Paul:

Don't worry about anything; instead, pray about everything. Tell God what you need, and thank him for all he has done. If you do this, you will experience God's peace, which is far more wonderful than the human mind can understand. His peace will guard your hearts and minds as you live in Christ Jesus. (Phil. 4:6-7)

But we have to make the choice not to look at the problem but to look at a person; his name is Jesus. Not only did David ask to be in God's presence, but he looked on God's perfection, to gaze upon the beauty of the Lord.

As we focus on who God is we see his faithfulness, his power, his love. David made a choice to seek God in his Temple.

The word 'seek' means to inquire or to petition. My son Jacob has just discovered the game of hide and seek. He loves running around the house shouting, 'Daddy, where are you?' I sometimes just leave enough of my body visible so he can find me easily. God is looking for people who will choose to search deeply for Him. And God always promises that if we genuinely seek Him we will always find Him.

David, this dynamic warrior who took on wild animals, who overcame giants and survived attacks on his life from the rulers of nations, is described as a 'man after God's heart'. He knew that spending time in God's presence focusing on what was real enabled him to overcome fear and become all that God had destined him to be.

Later when David was king, he passed on what he had learned to his people. He encouraged them to: 'Search for the LORD and for his strength, and keep on searching.' (1 Chr. 16:11)

Andy Booth

We'll be discovering what relying on the strength of God is all about in chapter 6, but for the moment we are going to conclude this chapter and discover what Jesus himself taught about worship.

Jesus had an amazing encounter with a Samaritan woman at a well. It was midday, the hottest time of the day, and she was there to draw water whilst no-one else was around. She was a bit of an outcast, but as usual that didn't bother Jesus. Before too long, she realized that Jesus was no ordinary man, and they began to talk about worship. Jesus gave her this great summary of why and how we worship:

'But the time is coming and is already here when true worshipers will worship the Father in spirit and in truth.

The Father is looking for anyone who will worship him that way. For God is Spirit, so those who worship him must worship in spirit and in truth.' (Jn. 4:23-24)

Jesus was saying in no uncertain terms to the woman that her worship was confused. He knew that like her ancestors, she was used to worshipping loads of false foreign gods as well as the one true God. Jesus wasn't saying that God was one spirit among many, but he was declaring that God is the one true spiritual being, who can give spiritual life to others.

Jesus also made it clear that the place of worship was meaningless, it was the reason for worship that was most important. True worship, said Jesus, means that you come openly, honestly and humbly before God.

The Samaritan woman had done the opposite and hadn't been able to open up her real self, her 'heart' to God. However, she must have been encouraged to hear that God was actively seeking true worshippers, because she soon expressed a desire to meet the Messiah, and once she realized exactly who Jesus was, she was desperate to introduce her friends to him with the words: 'Come and meet a man who told me everything I ever did! Can this be the Messiah?' (Jn. 4:29)

True worshippers of Jesus have a heart desire for others to worship him too. Do you?

3 FOLLOW THE MEN AND WOMEN OF GOD

Ant and Dec, Baddiel and Skinner, Trinny and Susannah: pairs of names that go together, friendships that are very public and have lasted the test of time. We'd all like a really good friend to go through life with – someone trustworthy and dependable. David found this type of person, and his name was Jonathan.

Jonathan was a brave young warrior. We first hear of him in the Bible as the winner of a great victory at a place called Gibeah that had been a Philistine stronghold. Jonathan was the eldest son of King Saul, which makes his friendship and loyalty to David astounding – but we'll discover all about that later in this chapter. For now we are going to concentrate on another bold victory that Jonathan achieved. He bravely decided to attack a Philistine outpost on his own – or at least just him and the very young guy carrying his armour:

> *Jonathan said to his young armour-bearer, 'Come, let's go over to the outpost of those uncircumcised fellows. Perhaps the LORD will act in our behalf. Nothing can hinder the LORD from saving, whether by many or by few.'*
>
> *'Do all that you have in mind,' his armour-bearer said. 'Go ahead; I am with you heart and soul.' (1 Sam. 14:6-7, NIV)*

This was how an extremely brave attack started. Two brave young men won a great victory against a large enemy army. I want you to put yourself in the position of Jonathan's armour carrier for a while, and imagine how you would have felt.

Your job was a responsible one because weapons and armour were precious and couldn't be lost. Not only that, you were carrying the armour that belonged to the king's son. A little bit of pressure so far! Then your boss decides to take you on a mission to spy on the enemy camp, and because it's risky business he doesn't tell his father.

When you are looking over the camp, Jonathan announces a plan to cross over to the enemy camp – perhaps the Lord would let you both taste a great victory against them.

As Jonathan unfolds his plan to you it seems pretty simple. If the enemy shouts, 'Come and have a go if you think you're hard enough!' then that will be the Lord's sign that they are ready for the taking!

Now think about the options before you. You could warn Jonathan about the risks, urge him to play safe in front of overwhelming odds, remind him that his dad would be furious and suggest he returns and get the rest of his forces. You could even tell him he's mad and do a runner out of there. You'd probably be risking your own job by doing any of those, but at least you wouldn't be rushing headlong into a fight with hundreds of Philistines.

Jonathan's armour-bearer chooses none of these options, but instead says 'Go ahead; I am with you heart and soul.' Other Bible translations say: 'I'm with you completely' (NLT) or 'I'm with you all the way' (*The Message*). And so he demonstrates to us another important spiritual lesson. Learning to follow the men and women of God – the people God has placed over us in leadership – is vital if we want to grow, take steps of faith and see God display his power.

Here's the result for Jonathan and his armour-bearer:

Jonathan said to his young armour-bearer, 'Come, let's go over to the outpost of those uncircumcised fellows. Perhaps the LORD *will act in our behalf. Nothing can hinder the* LORD *from saving, whether by many or by few.'*

> *'Do all that you have in mind,' his armour-bearer said. 'Go ahead; I am with you heart and soul.' (1 Sam. 14:6-7, NIV)*

Before too long the whole enemy camp was in panic, and Saul's lookout back at the Israelite camp spotted what was going on. Saul and his army assembled to fight but even before they got into battle they saw that the Philistines were mistakenly killing each other.

The Hebrew soldiers who had been fighting for the Philistines quickly rejoined the Israelite army, and they all helped run the Philistines out of the area. Jonathan and his armour-bearer took a small but very brave step, and from their small start a great victory was won. A few small but brave steps in your life could lead to a great spiritual triumph.

KEY VERSE

'Do all that you have in mind,' his armour-bearer said. 'Go ahead; I am with you heart and soul.' (1 Sam. 14:7, NIV)

On 28th May 1982, Lieutenant Colonel Jones was commanding 2nd battalion 'The Parachute' regiment on operations in the Falkland War. Fighting against heavily armed Argentinian forces, 'H' Jones as he was known saw that his troops were getting bogged down and in danger of losing an important battle. In the words of the official commendation that led to him receiving the Victoria Cross:

It was clear to him that desperate measures were needed in order to overcome the enemy position and rekindle the attack, and that unless these measures were taken promptly the battalion would sustain increasing casualties and the attack perhaps even fail. It was time for personal leadership and action. Colonel Jones immediately seized a sub-machine gun, and, calling on those around him and with total disregard for his own safety, charged the nearest enemy position. This action exposed him to fire from a number of trenches.

As he charged up a short slope at the enemy position he was seen to fall and roll backward downhill. He immediately picked himself up, and charged the enemy trench firing his sub-machine gun and seemingly oblivious to the intense fire directed at him. He was hit by fire from another trench that he outflanked and fell dying only a few feet from the enemy he had assaulted. A short time later a company of the battalion attacked the enemy, who quickly surrendered. The devastating display of courage by Colonel Jones had completely undermined their will to fight further.

Thereafter the momentum of the attack was rapidly regained, Darwin and Goose Green were liberated, and the battalion released the local inhabitants unharmed and forced the surrender of some 1,200 of the enemy... This was an action of the utmost gallantry by a commanding officer whose dashing leadership and courage throughout the battle were an inspiration to all about him.[1]

Many other leaders would have led from the back in this situation. It would have been acceptable for Colonel Jones to watch the battle through his binoculars a safe distance away, and let his junior officers lead the fight. He decided he would set the ultimate example and lead the 2nd battalion into their greatest challenge yet.

In fact, 'H' Jones was criticized by some experts for being too reckless, yet his troops followed his brave example and after his selfless death he was awarded the Victoria Cross, Britain's highest military honour.

It's good to follow

I wonder who your leaders are? Who could speak to you like Jonathan did? Is there someone in your life who could challenge you to join in doing something really brave? Would your reply be like Jonathan's armour-bearer? Just how obedient would you be?

The New Testament writer of the letter to the Hebrews recognized that it was important to follow the men and women of God when he wrote, 'Remember your leaders who first taught you the word of God. Think of all the good that has come from their lives, and trust the Lord as they do' (Heb. 13:7). *The Message* puts it like this:

> *Be responsive to your pastoral leaders. Listen to their counsel. They are alert to the condition of your lives and work under the strict supervision of God. Contribute to the joy of their leadership, not its drudgery. Why would you want to make things harder for them? (Heb. 13:17,* The Message*)*

Sometimes it's good to be a follower. It's like the story of a young woman who applied to go to Bible College. One of the questions on her application form asked 'Are you a leader?' Being honest, but also feeling like she'd blown her chances of going to the college, she replied 'no'.

She was amazed to receive a letter just a few days after she'd sent off her application which said: 'You have been accepted as a student of this college. When we checked all our application forms we saw that we would be having 150 leaders attending. We are letting you come to the college because all those leaders will need at least one follower.'

The three friendships everyone needs

If authority and accountability are issues for you then you definitely need these three types of people in your life:

- A Paul
- A Timothy
- A Barnabas

The Apostle Paul committed himself to help the younger Timothy to grow in his faith. In modern terms we would say he 'discipled' or 'mentored' Timothy. All along, Paul had a good friend and companion in Barnabas.

In his final days in a Roman prison cell, Paul chose to write to Timothy with some final words of encouragement and advice. Here he reminds him that they have a friendship and a relationship that is like father and son: *'You then, my son, be strong in the grace that is in Christ Jesus. And the things you have heard me say in the presence of many witnesses entrust to reliable men who will also be qualified to teach others.'* (2 Tim. 2:1-2, NIV)

When Timothy read this letter he would have remembered lots of shared experiences together: mission trips, miraculous conversions, preaching, arrests and plenty of signs of God at work. This long-lasting relationship was based on three things:

A relationship based on a positive choice

> *He came to Derbe and then to Lystra, where a disciple named Timothy lived, whose mother was a Jewess and a believer, but whose father was a Greek. The brothers at Lystra and Iconium spoke well of him. Paul wanted to take him along on the journey, so he circumcised him because of the Jews who lived in that area, for they all knew that his father was a Greek. As they travelled from town to town, they delivered the decisions reached by the apostles and elders in Jerusalem for the people to obey. So the churches were strengthened in the faith and grew daily in numbers. (Acts 16:1-5, NIV)*

It would have been easier for Paul to go it alone, but he wanted to take Timothy, to invest in him and to help him grow in ministry and maturity. It was a tough choice for Timothy to decide to travel with Paul. He had to get circumcised, so that his status as a Greek wouldn't offend the Jews he would be meeting. In effect, Timothy had to turn away from his own background and culture in order to learn from Paul. The result, however, was that the early church grew daily in numbers.

A relationship based over time

> *I thank God, whom I serve, as my forefathers did, with a clear conscience, as night and day I constantly remember you in my prayers. (2 Tim. 1:3, NIV)*

> *For this reason I remind you to fan into flame the gift of God, which is in you through the laying on of my hands. (2 Tim. 1:6, NIV)*

Paul had laid hands on Timothy right at the start of their time together, and now years later, he's still urging and reminding Timothy to use the gift that God has given him. Timothy by this time is probably a grown man in his late thirties or early forties and Paul is still desperate to see Timothy's destiny in God fulfilled.

I've found two modern examples of this type of relationship. The first is Jamie 'the naked chef' Oliver. In the project called 'Jamie's Kitchen' he took twelve disadvantaged young people to teach them all he knew about cooking, and to set them up for life as chefs.

By the end of the project, he had mortgaged his house to pay for the restaurant they were working in, spent hours and hours each day with them, got excited about their successes and upset with their failures. He'd given second and third chances, been let down and lied to, given countless master classes and eventually came out with a handful of top quality chefs. Jamie Oliver had invested a year of his time, money, energy, enthusiasm and knowledge into these young people.

The second example is the England rugby player Jonny Wilkinson. He says that wherever he goes in the world there are two older people he can always call on for advice, whatever time it is. He relies on fitness coach Steve Black for any concerns about training, fitness levels and injury, and if he just needs an encouraging conversation.

For the specialist coaching and advice he needs for kicking a rugby ball (and remember he's the man who won a rugby World Cup by kicking a drop goal), Jonny turns to kicking coach Dave Alred. Jonny says that even though he is an international superstar he still relies on the hours and hours of friendship and support that Black and Alred give him.

Of course these modern-day examples lack one crucial thing that Paul and Timothy had:

A relationship focused on Jesus

> *So you must never be ashamed to tell others about our Lord. And don't be ashamed of me, either, even though I'm in prison for Christ. With the strength God gives you, be ready to suffer with me for the proclamation of the Good News.*
>
> *It is God who saved us and chose us to live a holy life. He did this not because we deserved it, but because that was his plan long before the world began – to show his love and kindness to us through Christ Jesus. (2 Tim.1:8-9)*

In the first chapter of Paul's second letter to Timothy, we see the name of Jesus mentioned eight times in eighteen verses, and God the Father is mentioned eight times for good measure. So it's not just about following an older leader. It's about following a man or woman who is focused on God.

Think about what I am saying. The Lord will give you understanding in all these things. (2 Tim. 2:7)

And you should follow my example, just as I follow Christ's. (1 Cor. 11:1)

A good friend

In the early days after his conversion Paul was fortunate to have Barnabas vouch for him with the disciples. They were naturally suspicious of Paul, because he'd been a persecutor of Christians, but it was Barnabas who made sure that Paul was welcomed and accepted: 'Then Barnabas brought him to the apostles and told them how Saul had seen the Lord on the way to Damascus. Barnabas also told them what the Lord had said to Saul and how he boldly preached in the name of Jesus in Damascus.' (Acts 9:27)

Barnabas was just the type of reliable and honest friend that everyone needs: 'Barnabas was a good man, full of the Holy Spirit and strong in faith. And large numbers of people were brought to the Lord.' (Acts 11:24)

Honesty time

So here is an honesty moment for you.

- Do you have a Paul figure in your life? An older, more experienced Christian to help you grow?
- Do you have a Timothy figure in your life? A younger, less experienced Christian who you can help to grow?

Remember that you are never too old to need a Paul, and never too young to have a Timothy. And what about a Barnabas? A reliable friend who will be with you, and be honest with you, sharing the good times and the bad.

Maria Vincent was a very old lady when a doctor visited her small house in London. It was Victorian times, and Maria was extremely poor and extremely ill. She had no money for clothes, firewood or even food. The doctor was incensed that her friends could allow her to live like that, but when he asked the old lady about her friends he was disturbed to find that she had none.

A little later the old lady admitted that she did have one person who she could call a friend. When questioned by the doctor, she confessed that she had been a childhood friend of Queen Victoria herself. The doctor was not sure if he believed this story or not, but when he arrived home he sent a letter to the Queen explaining the situation.

It turned out that the story was true and Queen Victoria remembered Maria Vincent. The Queen sent a letter back to the caring doctor that included plenty of money to keep Maria comfortable for the rest of her life. Their childhood friendship had lasted a lifetime.[2]

REASONS I DON'T IGNITE

3. Isolation

One of the absolute basics of our faith is that we can't live it out in isolation. Followers of Jesus who attempt to follow without any depth of relationship with other Christians soon run out of steam. Now don't get me wrong; someone else can't live your life for you but they can give you the support, encouragement and friendship that you'll need. It's like the famous example of a burning coal going cold when it falls out of the fireplace, but remaining white hot when it's surrounded by other hot coals.

And if one falls down, the other helps,
But if there's no one to help, tough!

By yourself you're unprotected.
With a friend you can face the worst.
Can you round up a third?
A three-stranded rope isn't easily snapped. (Ecc. 4:10,12, The Message*)*

To remain on fire and really grow strong in faith you'll need to learn to follow the men and women of God and not be isolated. That means being open and honest, learning to trust other people by sharing your ups and your downs. Also remember that if you remain in isolation you are depriving other people of the support and friendship that you can offer!

Now that we're on the right track, let's stay on it. Stick with me, friends. Keep track of those you see running this same course, headed for this same goal. (Phil. 3:16-17, The Message*)*

Treat others with the faithful love of God

To round this chapter off, let's go back to the life of Jonathan. David and Jonathan had become great friends, but their friendship was being severely tested. It all revolved around the fact that Saul, Jonathan's father was very jealous of David.

Saul had given David the opportunity to marry his daughter Michal as long as he killed 100 Philistines. Saul expected David to get killed, but of course he managed to kill 200 Philistines just to prove himself. Saul's rage boiled over.

> *When the king realized how much the LORD was with David and how much Michal loved him, he became even more afraid of him, and he remained David's enemy for the rest of his life. Whenever the Philistine army attacked,*

David was more successful against them than all the rest of Saul's officers. So David's name became very famous throughout the land.

Saul now urged his servants and his son Jonathan to assassinate David. But Jonathan, because of his close friendship with David, told him what his father was planning. 'Tomorrow morning,' he warned him, 'you must find a hiding place out in the fields. I'll ask my father to go out there with me, and I'll talk to him about you. Then I'll tell you everything I can find out.' (1 Sam. 18:28-19:3)

Sure enough, Saul was determined to kill David. First Michal and then her brother Jonathan help David escape the evil plans of their father. Jonathan in particular took several dangerous risks to protect his friend David and they took a vow of friendship together: *'And Jonathan made a special vow to be David's friend.' (1 Sam. 18:3)*

When it came to the crunch many weaker friendships would have been shattered. At any time Jonathan could have told his father the king where David was, and David would have been assassinated. Remember that David had been chosen to be the next king, and that meant Jonathan, as the king's son, would miss out on the throne. If he'd been a jealous or a selfish friend, then David would have been a goner.

On the other hand, it was a long tradition that a new king would kill all the relatives of the previous king so that the relatives wouldn't try to revolt. Had David been a bitter person looking for revenge then Jonathan would have been doomed. Imagine the strain that the friendship must have been under. Right at the most stressful part Jonathan speaks:

Then Jonathan told David, 'I promise by the LORD, the God of Israel, that by this time tomorrow, or the next day at the latest, I will talk to my father and let you know at once how

> *he feels about you. If he speaks favorably about you, I will let you know. But if he is angry and wants you killed, may the* LORD *kill me if I don't warn you so you can escape and live. May the* LORD *be with you as he used to be with my father. And may you treat me with the faithful love of the* LORD *as long as I live. But if I die, treat my family with this faithful love, even when the Lord destroys all your enemies.'*
>
> *So Jonathan made a covenant with David, saying 'May the Lord destroy all your enemies!' And Jonathan made David reaffirm his vow of friendship again, for Jonathan loved David as much as he loved himself.* (1 Sam. 20:12-17)

The strength of their friendship not only ensured that David remained safe, but it also meant that he went on to treat Jonathan's family honourably, and later on actually welcomed Jonathan's crippled son, Mephibosheth, to eat with him at the king's table for as long as he lived. Wouldn't you want friends like David and Jonathan? People who would look out for you and protect you, people who would make sure that your family were looked after as well? That's friendship!

The great black American sprinter Jesse Owens told a story about when he was competing in the 1936 Olympics in Berlin. This was the Olympics that was supposed to show the world how great Nazi Germany was. Adolf Hitler himself was in the crowd. Owens was about to take part in the long jump; he was the world record holder but nevertheless very nervous. He noticed the German champion practising and jumping almost as far as his own world record; that made him even more nervous.

Hitler would want his champion to defeat the supposedly inferior black man, but the German champion decided to approach Owens and talk to him. Owens recalled that the German, called Luz Long, relaxed him with his conversation and made a helpful suggestion about Owen's first jump. Owen went onto win, break an Olympic record and get the second of four gold medals. When he had completed his winning jump, Owens was congratulated by Luz Long right in front of Adolf Hitler. Long and Owens never met again, as the German was killed in World War II, but Owens later wrote: 'You could melt down all the medals and cups I have, and they wouldn't be a plating on the 24-carat friendship I felt for Luz Long.'[3]

KEY VERSES

'And may you treat me with the faithful love of the LORD as long as I live.' (1 Sam. 20:14)

And Jonathan made David reaffirm his vow of friendship again, for Jonathan loved David as much as he loved himself. (1 Sam. 20:17)

4 OBEY THE COMMAND OF GOD

The army Sergeant Major barks the command out. To onlookers it sounds incomprehensible, but to the bunch of young recruits it has significance. They immediately obey his command and change the direction in which they are marching. At the shout of the next command, they stop and stand motionless, expectant, waiting for the Sergeant Major's voice to pierce the air once again.

Some people think God should be like that – shouting out commands from heaven that we are forced to obey. Yet that's not God's style at all. He wants our obedience, but he also wants us to want to be obedient. In chapter 2 we discovered loads of things about sacrifice and worship. Now we'll begin to discover that sacrifice is only worthwhile with an obedient heart. If we are constantly disobeying God then our worship and our sacrifice has little value.

Obedience issues

Almost from the word go, King Saul showed that he had obedience issues. Even before his jealousy of David, and Jonathan's determination to help his friend rather than his father, Saul was doing things his way rather than God's way.

In 1 Samuel chapter 13 we read of a time when Saul first led 3,000 specially selected troops from the Israelite army against a massive amount of Philistine warriors, chariots and horsemen. Saul's special troops weren't that special – they took one look at the numbers of Philistines against them and began to run away; in fact they tried to hide in caves, holes, rocks and water channels. Some escaped across the Jordan River, and Saul himself stayed at Gilgal with some men who were absolutely petrified.

Following some earlier instructions, Saul waited there for Samuel, but after seven days of waiting Saul got impatient:

> *Saul waited there seven days for Samuel, as Samuel had instructed him earlier, but Samuel still didn't come. Saul realized that his troops were rapidly slipping away. So he demanded, 'Bring me the burnt offering and the peace offerings!' And Saul sacrificed the burnt offering himself. Just as Saul was finishing with the burnt offering, Samuel arrived. Saul went out to meet and welcome him, but Samuel said, 'What is this you have done?'*
>
> *Saul replied, 'I saw my men scattering from me, and you didn't arrive when you said you would, and the Philistines are at Micmash ready for battle. So I said, "The Philistines are ready to march against us, and I haven't even asked for the LORD's help!" So I felt obliged to offer the burnt offering myself before you came.'*
>
> *'How foolish!' Samuel exclaimed. 'You have disobeyed the command of the LORD your God. Had you obeyed, the LORD would have established your kingdom over Israel forever. But now your dynasty must end, for the LORD has sought out a man after his own heart. The LORD has already chosen him to be king over his people, for you have not obeyed the LORD's command.' (1 Sam. 13:8-14)*

At first glance we read this and assume that Saul actually did a sensible thing. His troops were slipping off in different directions, and in order to keep them together he decided to sacrifice the burnt offering and the peace offering. The Philistines were gathering ready for a battle and Saul reckoned he desperately needed to seek God's favour and protection.

But Saul made two bad mistakes. First, he assumed that simply sacrificing animals would be enough to win God's approval, and second he had taken charge of a ritual that could only be performed with a prophet present. He hadn't waited for Samuel to show up.

For these mistakes, Saul was given a real telling off by Samuel, and even worse, he was rejected by God. Twice Samuel told Saul that he had disobeyed God, and he also broke the devastating news that had Saul been obedient, his dynasty (his family of royal rulers) would have lasted forever. Instead, the Lord had chosen someone with a heart like his own.

You would think that Saul would have learnt from this devastating situation, but sadly he didn't. Not long after Jonathan's brave attack on the Philistine camp, his father began to enjoy a period of strong military success. He was leading the Israelites to victory against their enemies in every direction. One day Samuel gave Saul a message from the Lord:

> *This is what the LORD Almighty says: 'I will punish the Amalekites for what they did to Israel when they waylaid them as they came up from Egypt. Now go, attack the Amalekites and totally destroy everything that belongs to them. Do not spare them; put to death men and women, children and infants, cattle and sheep, camels and donkeys.' (1 Sam. 15:2-3, NIV)*

What a tough message to deliver, and what a tough command to carry out. Yet Saul was used to wars and soon mobilized his army ready to fight. His troops had no problem in slaughtering and destroying everyone and everything that came in their path. However, remember that Saul wasn't an obedient man, and so he not only spared the life of the Amalekite king Agag, but he also kept the best sheep, calves and lambs for himself and his men.

In fact the story says that they only destroyed what was of poor quality or worthless. Saul had already thrown his royal succession away and now found himself in another mess. Dishonest and disobedient people begin to believe their own lies and alienate themselves from God, but in the end the truth always wins.

How foolish Saul must have been to think that he could get away with this disobedience and that God wouldn't find out: *'Then the LORD said to Samuel, "I am sorry that I ever made Saul king, for he has not been loyal to me and has again refused to obey my command." Samuel was so deeply moved when he heard this that he cried out to the LORD all night.' (1 Sam. 15:10-11)*

From bad to worse

This was a serious incident! Saul's disobedience had made God regret appointing him as king, and had made Samuel so upset that he spent all night crying out to God. Samuel determined to go and find Saul and confront him, and as he travelled to find Saul he discovered that Saul was building himself a monument to celebrate his victory. Saul was going from bad to worse: not content in being disobedient he was now claiming all the honour and glory for himself and not for the Lord.

When Samuel eventually caught up with the king, Saul tried to pretend that nothing was wrong and said, 'I have carried out the Lord's command.' Samuel was no fool, and quickly asked Saul about the animal noises that they could both hear. Saul continued to dig a hole for himself by replying that he and his men intended to sacrifice the animals to the Lord, and that they had destroyed everything else. He was trying to blame his men for the decision he himself had taken.

By this time Samuel had heard enough and he told Saul exactly what the Lord had revealed to him the night before. Saul still insisted that he had been obedient, and then Samuel replied:

> *'What is more pleasing to the LORD: your burnt offerings and sacrifices or your obedience to his voice? Obedience is far better than sacrifice. Listening to him is much better than offering the fat of rams. Rebellion is as bad as the sin of witchcraft, and stubbornness is as bad as worshiping idols. So because you have rejected the word of the LORD, he has rejected you from being king.'* (1 Sam. 15:22-23)

Telling it as it really is

Samuel got straight to the heart of the issue and told it to Saul as it really was. God is always more concerned about his people being obedient to his voice rather than just offering sacrifices. It was a hard lesson for Saul to hear, but eventually he admitted that he had ignored Samuel's message and disobeyed God's command. His confession came too late though, because not only had his family lost the right to succeed him as ruler, the Lord had also rejected him as king of Israel.

Saul's foolishness reminds me of this story. On a winter ski resort there was a sign near a certain slope saying, 'Danger. Keep Out'. Unfortunately, many people disobeyed the sign and went to ski on the dangerous slope. Before too long an avalanche struck and four foolish skiers died. The cost of being obedient is nothing compared to the cost of being disobedient.

KEY VERSE

But Samuel replied, 'What is more pleasing to the LORD: your burnt offerings and sacrifices or your obedience to his voice? Obedience is far better than sacrifice. Listening to him is much better than offering the fat of rams.' (1 Sam. 15:22)

Edward VI was King of England in the sixteenth century. He was known for often going to church and standing up to listen to the Bible being read. More than that, he would write down notes on the reading and would refer to these notes during the rest of the week. He didn't just want to understand the word of God more fully; he was desperate to apply it to his everyday life. The king recognized that a simple step of obedience was worth much more than any of his studying.[4]

REASONS I DON'T IGNITE

4: Independence

One of the most important things to grasp about following Jesus is that he is in charge. That's what the phrase 'Jesus is Lord' means, and that's why the earliest Christians used the phrase as a central part of their belief and repeated it to each other again and again. Being a real disciple means handing over our independence and allowing Jesus to be in control: 'Then he told them what they could expect for themselves: "Anyone who intends to come with me has to let me lead. You're not in the driver's seat – I am. Don't run from suffering; embrace it. Follow me and I'll show you how."' (Lk. 9:23, *The Message*)

Whenever we insist on making our own decisions, stating our rights or openly disobeying what we know God wants, we are in effect rejecting Jesus as Lord. We can be sure that God won't stop loving us, but he will be saddened and there may be consequences for us just like there were for Saul.

Don't you realize that you become the slave of whatever you choose to obey? You can choose sin, which leads to death, or you can choose to obey God and receive his approval. (Rom. 6:16)

Once again, the Apostle Paul knew what it meant to surrender his independence:

> *Christ's life showed me how, and enabled me to do it. I identified myself completely with him. Indeed, I have been crucified with Christ. My ego is no longer central. It is no longer important that I appear righteous before you or have your good opinion, and I am no longer driven to impress God. Christ lives in me. The life you see me living is not 'mine,' but it is lived by faith in the Son of God, who loved me and gave himself for me. (Gal. 2:20,* The Message*)*

George Muller was a man who trusted the Lord. He was born in 1805 and he is remembered as both an English evangelist and philanthropist. A man of faith and prayer, he established orphanages in Bristol and founded the Scriptural Knowledge Institution for Home and Abroad. Muller estimated that Christ answered 50,000 of his prayers.

He was once asked the secret behind his service, as it was widely known that God had continually met the needs of the orphanage without Muller making them known. How did he exist like this? Muller replied: 'There was a day when I died, utterly died.'

As he spoke, he bent lower and lower until he almost touched the floor, displaying his submission before God. 'I died to George Muller, his opinions, his preferences, tastes, and will,' he explained. 'I died to the approval or blame even of my brethren and friends. And since then, I have studied only to show myself approved unto God.'[5]

Hard work or heart work?

In the New Living Translation, there are over 350 references to obedience, and the Bible is littered with verses that echo the theme of obedience being better than sacrifice. They confirm to us that obedience to God shouldn't be hard work but should be heart work:

You would not be pleased with sacrifices, or I would bring them.
If I brought you a burnt offering, you would not accept it.
The sacrifice you want is a broken spirit.
A broken and repentant heart,
O God, you will not despise. (Ps. 51:16-17)

The Lord *is more pleased when we do what is right and just than when we give him sacrifices.* (Prov. 21:3)

These verses remind us that whilst God isn't against sacrifice, and actually welcomes it, he is much more concerned about our heart attitude. Our inner commitment and love for God is much more important than any outward show that we might make. Humility, repentance, right attitude towards God – these are the keys to God's pleasure, not empty offerings that aren't backed up by our real feelings. One Bible commentary on Proverbs 21 that I read stated that God has a 'priority of righteousness':

The Lord requires righteousness before religious service. Doing 'what is right and just' is more acceptable to the Lord than sacrifice. It does not teach that ritual acts of worship are to be avoided; rather, it stresses that religious acts are valueless without righteous living.[6]

Isn't that a great phrase? A priority of righteousness! Even as I'm writing, I'm being challenged by how often that is the real priority of my daily life. How about you?

Unfortunately, throughout the history of God's people, this priority of righteousness hasn't always been top of the agenda. Time and again, God's representatives have had to give urgent warnings. Here are God's words spoken through the prophet Jeremiah:

> *'This is what I told them: "Obey me, and I will be your God, and you will be my people. Only do as I say, and all will be well!"*
>
> *'But my people would not listen to me. They kept on doing whatever they wanted, following the stubborn desires of their evil hearts. They went backward instead of forward.' (Jer. 7:23-24)*

Jeremiah is reminding the Israelites that God demanded obedience from them when he gave them the Ten Commandments, but that sadly this was the main thing lacking in the people.

When we arrive at the New Testament we discover that as far as sacrifice is concerned, Jesus has made the once and for all sacrifice on our behalf, and that holiness comes from Jesus and not from any sacrifice we can make: 'And what God wants is for us to be made holy by the sacrifice of the body of Jesus Christ once for all time.' (Heb. 10:10)

What's in it for us?

No sacrifice that we make can ever match up to Jesus' sacrificial death on the cross, but what we do have to offer is our heartfelt worship, love and obedience. Even when Jesus offers forgiveness to an adulterous woman in John's Gospel, part of the deal is that she becomes obedient and doesn't continue in a life that dishonours God. She can accomplish this not through extravagant sacrifice but by following Jesus:

Then Jesus stood up again and said to her, 'Where are your accusers? Didn't even one of them condemn you?'

'No, Lord,' she said.

And Jesus said, 'Neither do I. Go and sin no more.'

Jesus said to the people, 'I am the light of the world. If you follow me, you won't be stumbling through the darkness, because you will have the light that leads to life.' (Jn. 8:10-12)

Jesus was teaching her a lesson that he consistently taught his followers: true discipleship is displayed by obedience. Those of us who claim to love Jesus will want to demonstrate that by our obedience to him:

Jesus replied, 'All those who love me will do what I say. My Father will love them, and we will come to them and live with them. Anyone who doesn't love me will not do what I say. And remember, my words are not my own. This message is from the Father who sent me.' (Jn. 14:23-24)

Now please, please, don't get this wrong. I'm not saying that for God to love us we must be obedient! I am saying that in response to God's great love for us we will want to demonstrate our love and gratitude back by being obedient.

Peter explains to us, in the first chapter of his letter, just where our obedience fits in to God's plan, and what incredible reward we receive for it: *'God the Father chose you long ago, and the Spirit has made you holy. As a result, you have obeyed Jesus Christ and are cleansed by his blood. May you have more and more of God's special favor and wonderful peace.' (1 Pet. 1:2)*

Honesty time

Have an honesty moment before God now as you consider the following questions. Take time to think them through.

- How do you practise obedience?
- In what areas do you struggle to obey God?
- Have you ever doubted that God's plan is the best for you?
- How will you begin to follow Jesus with heart work and not hard work?

I've asked Andy Booth to help us out again, and he's going to get personal about obedience.

IS OBEYING GOD THE KEY TO HIM LIKING US?

So much of our energy each day is directed towards acting in such a way that people will like us and approve of us. I have been a musician most of my life and have often fallen in the trap of trying to perform so that people would like me. When I played well, people would come and tell me how much they liked it and I would feel good, but even with all the words of encouragement there would often be times when I would still feel empty inside. It is easy to look at God in the same way, assuming that it is only when we have become the perfect Christian that he will really like us.

What does God really think about us? Read how God describes his love for the people of Israel: **'The Lord did not choose you and lavish his love on you because you were larger or greater than other nations, for you were the smallest of all nations!'** (Deut. 7:7)

Do you notice that God doesn't say he loves his people because of how significant or important they are; he loves them because he chooses to love them! It is about his choice, not our behaviour. As my colleague, Ron Allen at Heartland Church says, 'We have to move from doing things for God to gain his approval, to living for him out of the approval he has already shown us.'

It was not until I understood God's unconditional love for me that the layers of performance started to strip away from my heart and mind. A few years ago I was involved in representing Wales at a large event at Wembley Stadium called 'Champion of the World'. There were 50-60,000 people there and it was an amazing feeling to be speaking to that many people about what God was doing in Wales. During that time I was also working in a nursing home.

In the middle of my next shift after that big event I was helping to take an elderly man to the bathroom when I sensed God's presence even more than when I was speaking at Wembley. I felt like God was teaching me that as we understand how God sees us – as one of his children – it doesn't matter whether what he asks us to do impacts thousands or the person in front of you: the key is obedience.

If there is nothing we can do to make God love us more, then the stress of trying to please him based on our performance is taken away. From there you can get involved with what God is already doing, and obedience becomes an adventure.

Andy Booth

God's way is always the best way

It's amazing how so many of us don't always believe that if we are obedient to God it will be the best thing we can ever do. God's plans and purposes give us more fulfilment and happiness than we could ever hope to obtain by being disobedient. Even when being obedient to God's commands is tough and costly it is still the best thing to do!

If there was ever someone who had walked this earth and would have been justified in doing his own thing it was Jesus; but he consistently reminded everyone around him that his purpose was to be obedient to his heavenly father: *'For I have come down from heaven to do the will of God who sent me, not to do what I want.' (Jn. 6:38)*

If Jesus' priority was to be obedient to God, then don't you think ours should be too? Even in those dark moments at the Mount of Olives on the night before he was going to be crucified, Jesus focused on being obedient. Even though he was finding his mission really tough he could say: *'Father, if you are willing, please take this cup of suffering away from me. Yet I want your will, not mine.' (Lk. 22:42)*

That's one of the secrets of being obedient to God highlighted right there: to be able to honestly say to him, 'Whatever it takes, Lord, I want to do what you think is best, not what I think is best.'

HOW DO WE HEAR THE COMMAND OF GOD?

You might be saying to yourself, 'Well, it's one thing to be obedient to God when you know what he wants you to do, but quite another to discover what God's command is in the first place.' Remember in chapter 1 how we learnt about the ways in which God speaks to us? Below are some of the ways that God will speak to you and give you guidance and direction. Every now and then you'll hear such a clear command from God that you know you can't do anything but obey.

You'll hear God's command in some of the following ways:

- *In the Bible.* One easy way of discovering if you are living in disobedience to God is if your life goes against biblical teaching. God will never ask you to do something that is the opposite of his character and his values which are shown in Scripture.
- *Through prayer.* If you genuinely come to God with an honest and open heart, then you'll be ready to receive correction and guidance and you'll be sensitive enough to realize it's God speaking to you.
- *Through the Holy Spirit.* He will heighten your conscience and you'll know deep down inside that God is giving you a clear command. It might be to stop doing something that dishonours him, or it may be to accept a call to serve him powerfully. Whatever it is, you won't be peaceful inside until you obey.
- *Through other Christians.* Your church leaders and older trusted friends will often be used by God to speak his words into your life. Perhaps you've been in a church service and it felt like the speaker was directing all his comments personally to you! That's sometimes how God gets our attention.

Be open to hearing God, and when you hear him, obey!

5 SEE WITH THE VISION OF GOD

Imagine what would happen if a talent scout for rugby players went to watch a match in a small South Wales village. Wales are in need of a new captain for their team and the talent scout has heard that the local farmer has seven talented sons playing in the village team. During the first half of the game, the farmer points out his three oldest sons one at a time, but the talent scout isn't interested. So in the second half the farmer highlights his youngest three sons, but still the talent scout hasn't found the player he is looking for.

With only a few minutes left on the clock, the team brings on a replacement – it is the farmer's eighth son, a handsome boy but so small and insignificant that his dad didn't even mention him. 'That's him,' the talent scout cries out. 'He's the one I'm after!'

I've made that story up, and it's completely over the top isn't it? Yet something very similar happened when Samuel anointed the new king of Israel.

Eventually, the relationship between Samuel and Saul was damaged beyond repair, and the Lord made plans for Israel to move on:

> *Samuel never went to meet with Saul again, but he mourned constantly for him. And the* LORD *was sorry he had ever made Saul king of Israel.*
>
> *Finally, the* LORD *said to Samuel, 'You have mourned long enough for Saul. I have rejected him as king of Israel. Now fill your horn with olive oil and go to Bethlehem. Find a man named Jesse who lives there, for I have selected one of his sons to be my new king.'* (1 Sam. 15:35-16:1)

When Samuel saw Jesse's family he assumed that the oldest and tallest son would be the one that God had chosen to be king. Instead, Samuel learnt a valuable lesson about the difference between the way humans look at people and judge them, and the way that God examines and judges:

> *When they arrived, Samuel took one look at Eliab and thought ,'Surely this is the LORD's anointed!' But the LORD said to Samuel, 'Don't judge by his appearance or height, for I have rejected him. The LORD doesn't make decisions the way you do! People judge by outward appearance, but the LORD looks at a person's thoughts and intentions.' (1 Sam. 16:6-7)*

So Eliab had been rejected, and the very same process went on through Abinadab, Shammah, and the other four sons. Samuel was concerned, and asked Jesse if he had any more sons:

> *Then Samuel asked, 'Are these all the sons you have?'*
>
> *'There is still the youngest,' Jesse replied. 'But he's out in the fields watching the sheep.'*
>
> *'Send for him at once,' Samuel said. 'We will not sit down to eat until he arrives.'*
>
> *So Jesse sent for him. He was ruddy and handsome, with pleasant eyes. And the LORD said, 'This is the one; anoint him.'*
>
> *So as David stood there among his brothers, Samuel took the olive oil he had brought and poured it on David's head. And the Spirit of the LORD came mightily upon him from that day on. Then Samuel returned to Ramah. (1 Sam. 16:11-13)*

A day of destiny

This was a momentous day for David. We can view it with the benefit of hindsight and remember all the great things David was going to accomplish, but everyone involved in this scene must have been staggered when David was chosen as the future king. Even Samuel would have been amazed as he anointed the young David. Only the Lord saw potential and destiny in the little shepherd boy David. It wasn't as if the spirit of the Lord had powerfully been on David much before this, because we are told that the Spirit of the Lord came mightily upon him 'from that day on'.

Here was David – the youngest, the smallest, the least significant, the least appreciated of all the brothers – carrying out the simplest and least important job of looking after the sheep. Yet God has seen something special in David. It's as if what you do isn't as important as the way you do it. We live in a world where it always seems to be about ability, but God chose David based on character.

When Samuel sent for David, the young man was exactly where they would all have expected him to be: out in the fields faithfully looking after the sheep. When David arrived, the gathered crowd of people weren't even sitting down relaxed; they were standing to wait for him. It's as if God was saying, 'Jesse's older sons are big guys, they've got some great talent and ability. They really look good, but I've had my eye on them all when no-one else was watching; I've spotted the one who has what it takes on the inside to be my king.' With David's heart God could add his own spirit and power, and accomplish great things.

Why me?

I'm not for a moment trying to liken myself to David, but every time I hear this story I'm reminded of a situation from my own youth. When I was a young guy of eleven, I moved up from one age range in the youth group to the next. There were eight of us all around eleven and twelve; we were the youngest in the older age range. Often we would all stand in a line. I was the smallest of the youngest! (Most of those around my age stayed in the youth group for the next few years and gradually I grew a bit and wasn't always the smallest.)

However, as I look back I'm reminded that of all the guys in that line – even out of almost all the older ones too – I'm the only person still going on with the Lord and involved in Christian ministry. I often ask myself 'Why me?' I certainly wasn't the biggest, or the cleverest, or even the most spiritually aware, but I guess God saw something in me.

If you had asked one of the youth leaders to name one young person for future leadership I bet my name would not have been uttered! I've never got anywhere near being the great leader David was, but I've made a few of the same mistakes.

What about you?

Put yourself in David's position. What would have been going through his mind when he was being anointed by Samuel? How would you have felt? Afraid? Excited? Big-headed? Not really understanding what was going on? I wonder how often David looked back to that day with humility and thanksgiving to God.

David's future included a great victory against Goliath, a victory over all the Philistines, a lifelong friendship with Jonathan, a career as a prolific writer of Psalms, the rescuer of the Ark of the Covenant and an overall reign as king that lasted for forty years.

Yet we'd be wrong if we thought that David was the perfect superstar who never made a mistake. God knows everything and works throughout time – past, present and future. So on the day that David was anointed, the Lord not only knew the great accomplishments that David would enjoy, he also knew the mistakes and failings that David would succumb to.

In a moment of great weakness as king, David committed adultery with Bathsheba and organized a conspiracy so that her husband Uriah the Hittite would die in the front line of battle. As a result, God had to discipline David, and so his illegitimate child born out of adultery died.

When God chose David, he chose someone with a great future, with immense potential to serve the Lord. The Spirit of the Lord was upon David; but God didn't choose someone who was perfect and who was destined never to make a mistake.

In fact much later on in his life David tried to act without God's authority when he attempted to take a military survey of Israel, and again God was displeased.

Despite this there are over fifty references in the Bible to the love and faithfulness that David displays towards the Lord, and his name becomes a prophetic name for Jesus Christ.

KEY VERSE

'The LORD doesn't make decisions the way you do! People judge by outward appearance, but the LORD looks at a person's thoughts and intentions.' (1 Sam. 16:7)

Popular choice or God's choice?

Saul had been the popular choice for king but David was God's choice. Saul would have been the obvious choice to tackle the giant Goliath, but he didn't have the faith in his heart that David had. One of Saul's other big problems was that he couldn't seem to see things from God's perspective.

Where God hoped Saul would see a reason to serve, Saul instead saw an opportunity for selfishness. When Saul should have shown humility, he was chasing fame and praise. When he could have demonstrated generosity Saul preferred to be greedy. Saul's priorities were so often wrong, and that was because he was used to seeing things his way and didn't really learn to see with the vision of God.

Both Samuel and David were taught a valuable lesson when David was anointed as king. God was demonstrating to them what the Apostle Paul would call 'walking by faith' and 'not by sight', or living by believing and not seeing. All of us get caught up in the circumstances around us and base our thinking and our decisions purely on the superficial way that things seem to be right now.

God operates a different system. He looked at David, and saw a young man whom he later described as 'a man after my own heart' (Acts 13:22) rather than simply seeing David as he was at the time – small, young, inexperienced and seemingly insignificant.

One of the favourite projects that I'm involved with at Ignite in Cardiff is the Ignite Leadership Academy. Once or twice a year we take fifteen young people who, we believe, have some leadership potential and we give them the opportunity to learn and grow.

There is often surprise at the young men and women we accept onto the Leadership Academy. Their parents still see them as troublesome teenagers, their church leaders haven't spotted any potential in them yet and think they are too young, and even the young people themselves lack confidence and don't always believe in themselves as potential leaders. Yet we try to see them as God sees them – examining their heart and looking to who they can be, rather than just who they are now.

Going for gold

Steve Redgrave, the five times Olympic gold medal winning rower, tells the story of when he was selected in 1978 to row for the British junior team for the first time in the World Championships. He was a year younger than the other boys selected, and when two of the boys out of the four heard that a younger, unknown, untried, inexperienced rower had been selected they withdrew from the boat saying they didn't want to row with a no-hoper! Steve goes on to say that somewhere now there must be two men aged forty or so kicking themselves at being so stupid.[7]

I believe with all my heart that God never looks down on you in the same judgemental way that those two boys viewed Steve Redgrave. Never does God say you are too young, or too inexperienced, or that you are a nobody with no hope. In fact, God says exactly the opposite.

Good news or bad news?

Of course, the fact that God looks at the heart and not at outward appearance can be both good news and bad news. For those of us who may not always look the part outwardly but have a heart that is turned towards God, we can take comfort from the way that God measures people. For those of us who outwardly say and do all the right things but whose heart is more concerned with ourselves rather than the Lord, his standards of judgement and vision are a caution. God never confuses appearance with reality, and we should learn to do the same.

Above all, the story of Samuel choosing and anointing David should give us the confidence to dream dreams, to refuse to accept things just as they are and to begin to see through God's eyes rather than our own. God's ways will never simply be the ways that the world has always done things, and he will always see potential and destiny for us when those around us might reject us.

Dreaming with destiny

It started like so many evenings. Jimmy's mum and dad were at home and Jimmy was playing after dinner. His mum and dad were absorbed with jobs and did not notice the time. It was a full moon and some of the light seeped through the windows. Then Jimmy's mum glanced at the clock. 'Jimmy, it's time to go to bed. Go up now and I'll come and settle you later.'

Unusually, Jimmy went straight upstairs to his room. An hour or so later his mother came up to check if all was well, and to her astonishment found that her son was staring quietly out of his window at the moonlit scenery.

'What are you doing, Jimmy?'

'I'm looking at the moon, mummy.'

'Well, it's time to go to bed now.'

As one reluctant boy settled down, he said, 'Mummy, you know one day I'm going to walk on the moon.' Who could have known that the boy with the dream that night would survive a near fatal motorbike crash which broke almost every bone in his body? Who could have known that James Irwin would fulfil this dream thirty-two years later when he stepped on the moon's surface, just one of the twelve representatives of the human race to have done so?[8]

See others the way God sees them

When you begin to see with the vision of God, it doesn't just change the way you see yourself, it changes the way you see other people around you. This was a lesson that David learnt and put into practice later on in his life. In 1 Samuel chapter 24 David was hiding in the wilderness because Saul, overcome with jealousy, was out to kill him. Saul chose 3,000 men to accompany him on a mission to hunt David down and kill him.

Whilst they were searching, Saul went into a cave to go to the toilet. Completely unknown to him, David and his men were hiding in the very same cave. David's men tried to convince David to seek revenge against Saul, but all David did was to secretly cut a piece of cloth from Saul's robe. Even then David felt guilty about his action:

> *'The LORD knows I shouldn't have done it,' he said to his men. 'It is a serious thing to attack the LORD's anointed one, for the LORD himself has chosen him.' So David sharply rebuked his men and did not let them kill Saul.*
>
> *After Saul had left the cave and gone on his way, David came out and shouted after him, 'My LORD the king!' And when Saul looked around, David bowed low before him.*
>
> *Then he shouted to Saul, 'Why do you listen to the people who say I am trying to harm you? This very day you can see with your own eyes it isn't true. For the LORD placed you at my mercy back there in the cave, and some of my men told me to kill you, but I spared you. For I said, "I will never harm him – he is the LORD's anointed one."' (1 Sam. 24:6-10)*

Even though David's life had been in danger from Saul, David wasn't prepared to take revenge. His men were ready to kill Saul because they saw the situation purely from a human perspective. David, on the other hand, was beginning to see with godly vision and was applying godly judgement to the situation rather than his own.

The eyes of Jesus

Throughout the gospels we can see Jesus looking at people and situations in completely different ways from those around him. When we look at Jesus, because he is God personified, we can see how God looks at the world.

In Luke's Gospel alone, Jesus had encounters with all types of people who were looked at with distaste and even hatred by others. He let a sinful woman kiss his feet and pour expensive oil on his head when the Pharisees had nothing but contempt for her. They called her a sinner; Jesus forgave her sins. Jesus knew that 5,000 could be fed with the packed lunch of a young boy, whilst the disciples thought that everyone would starve.

Jesus saw a group of parents bringing their children to see him, and when the disciples told them not to bother him, Jesus taught the disciples an important lesson on receiving the Kingdom of God like little children. Jesus saw the unpopular Zacchaeus, a corrupt tax collector, and was willing to meet with him as a guest in his house.

When Jesus came close to Jerusalem in the final days before his crucifixion, he took a look at the city and began to cry because of its desperate spiritual state and the violent future it was going to have.

Even on the cross, Jesus was able to look at those who were crucifying him and ask God to forgive them. He looked at a repentant criminal, being executed next to him, and assured him that he would be in paradise.

REASONS I DON'T IGNITE

5. Ignorance

Such stupidity and ignorance! Their eyes are closed, and they cannot see. Their minds are shut, and they cannot think. (Is. 44:18)

When God offers us the opportunity to see ourselves, to see others and to see the world as he sees them, we must take every opportunity to do just that. If we keep on trying to use our own worldly vision then we'll never grow in our faith. We will remain ignorant and spiritually short-sighted. Of course we can never fully understand the extravagant wisdom and insight of the Lord Almighty, but God does want us to rely on him and not on our own knowledge.

This is how Isaiah prophesied about Jesus:

> *And the Spirit of the LORD will rest on him – the Spirit of wisdom and understanding, the Spirit of counsel and might, the Spirit of knowledge and the fear of the LORD. He will delight in obeying the LORD. He will never judge by appearance, false evidence or hearsay. He will defend the poor and the exploited. He will rule against the wicked and destroy them with the breath of his mouth. He will be clothed with fairness and truth. (Is. 11:2-5)*

Wouldn't you want to be like that? You might feel like the writer of Proverbs when he says:

> *I am too ignorant to be human, and I lack common sense. I have not mastered human wisdom, nor do I know the Holy One. (Prov. 30:2)*

Be assured that if you genuinely seek God's perspective and God's wisdom then he will give it to you. Keep praying to see with the vision of God and you'll be amazed at the spiritual insight, compassion and wisdom that God will equip you with.

It's time to ask Andy Booth to give us some sensible and helpful advice:

SEEING THINGS GOD'S WAY

Let me give you some practical ways of dealing with challenging situations, and getting God's perspective on them. Just like a laser burns an image onto a CD, so what we look at will stick into our minds for a long time. So how should we respond to the following?

It's time to have an **honesty moment** about three key areas:

- **Lust**. Someone once said that it is not wrong to look at a bird flying over your head, but it is a sin to let a bird make a nest in your hair! We all have to make choices about what we look at.

PRACTICAL TIP: If you struggle with lust when you look at a certain person, maybe it's a person in your school or church, or even someone on TV, then try this exercise. Every day for 30 days ask God to show you how he sees that person. When you see that person, pray that same prayer. You will notice that God will change the way you see that person from an object of desire to a precious child of God.

- **Anger.** If I were to ask you who annoyed you the most, whose name comes in to your head? It probably didn't take very long to think of the person who really has hurt you.

PRACTICAL TIP: Start by remembering how much God has forgiven you. When we feel as if we are not forgiven we can be unforgiving towards others, but God will never ask us to forgive other people more than he has forgiven us. Then make the choice to stop playing back situations in your mind from the past. Whenever we do that, it makes it easier for anger and bitterness to grow inside us. Ask God to show you his heart for that person. Then choose to forgive them.

One day Peter asked Jesus how much he should forgive. Expecting to impress Jesus, Peter asks 'Seven times?' Jesus replied 'Seventy times seven times'. Jesus is basically saying that if we are counting how much we forgive, it doesn't really count.

There will be times when you need to forgive time and time again because emotions follow decisions. It might take time for the pain to subside, so when you feel the anger rise up inside, you need to be ruthless with it and forgive that person again immediately.

- **Situations of injustice and pain.** Jesus was constantly seeing situations of pain, being moved by situations of pain, and then doing something about situations of pain.

PRACTICAL TIP: When we pray for a situation of need, we have to be willing to be part of the answer to our own prayers. The disciples were the answer to their own prayers! Think about the pain and injustice around you, a person getting bullied at school, a friend whose parents are struggling with a divorce. How do we respond?

First, ask God to show you where the need is around you. Ask him to point out situations and people you have never noticed before. Then pray for those people and situations: ask God to fill your heart with compassion. The word compassion is where we get the phrase 'I'm gutted'. It means to feel something really deeply in the depths of our body.

The King James Version of the Bible translates the word compassion as 'bowels of mercy'.[9] When God fills you with compassion, ask him to show you how you can be part of the answer to your own prayers to see him move in that situation. Be bold and do everything he asks you to do as you begin to see things through his eyes.

Andy Booth

6 RELY ON THE STRENGTH OF GOD

Has there ever been a fight like it? Forget about Mike Tyson versus Lennox Lewis or Mohammed Ali versus Joe Frazier for those of you old enough to recall. The World Wrestling Federation had Hulk Hogan and Sergeant Slaughter, plus all the loud music and razzamatazz, but still that pales into insignificance.

The fight I'm referring to was the most famous one-on-one encounter in all of history. To this day, every sports commentator mentions this fight when commenting on a big fish taking on a minnow. Whenever there is a huge upset, and the underdog beats the champion, then this fight is remembered. We're talking about David and Goliath.

The lead up to the big fight

Here's the scene. David has been anointed as the next king of Israel but he hasn't become king yet. In fact he's been summoned to King Saul's court to be a harp player. Soon after this, the armies of Israel and Philistine find themselves face to face on opposite hills, ready for battle.

Nine feet tall Goliath was the Philistine champion, and in those days you could avoid whole armies fighting by having the best fighter in each participating in a winner-takes-all contest. The only problem with this solution was that no-one from the Israelite army fancied taking on Goliath one little bit:

> *Goliath stood and shouted across to the Israelites, 'Do you need a whole army to settle this? Choose someone to fight for you, and I will represent the Philistines. We will settle*

this dispute in single combat! If your man is able to kill me, then we will be your slaves. But if I kill him, you will be our slaves! I defy the armies of Israel! Send me a man who will fight with me!' When Saul and the Israelites heard this, they were terrified and deeply shaken. (1 Sam. 17:8-11)

Now David was only on the battlefield to deliver supplies. His three oldest brothers had joined Saul's army and David was travelling back and forth between helping his dad with the sheep and working for Saul.

One day, David's father asked him to deliver some food to his brothers and David arrives at the front line in time to see Goliath strutting his stuff. In fact Goliath had been parading up and down in front of the Israelite army for forty days, twice a day – morning and evening.

In Scripture the period of forty days is often used to describe a time of testing, a difficult make or break period, and this was certainly the case here. This was the daily response: 'As soon as the Israelite army saw him, they began to run away in fright. "Have you seen the giant?" the men were asking.' (1 Sam. 17:24-25a)

A person of faith is always on duty

One thing you should know about 'little' David: he'd arrived at the battle with a few victories already. He'd fought mountain bears and won, he'd snatched a lamb from the jaws of a lion, and pretty soon it was obvious that he wasn't going to be content simply bringing supplies to the army – as far as he was concerned he was on duty and he was ready to fight.

Before too long, David volunteered to take on Goliath and did so with the confidence that God would be with him: 'The LORD who saved me from the claws of the lion and the bear will save me from this Philistine!'

> *Saul finally consented. 'All right, go ahead,' he said. 'And may the* Lord *be with you!' (1 Sam. 17:37)*

What did David carry into battle with him?

David certainly carried with him the faith that God would prevail; he'd been reliant on God when he fought the bears and the lions, so this would be no different. Yet he also carried with him the negative views of his brothers. Before Saul agreed to let David fight, this is what David's oldest brother thought:

> *But when David's oldest brother, Eliab, heard David talking to the men, he was angry. 'What are you doing around here anyway?' he demanded. 'What about those few sheep you're supposed to be taking care of? I know about your pride and dishonesty. You just want to see the battle!' (1 Sam. 17:28)*

King Saul's view of David was hardly any better. Just before the king realized that he was so desperate and afraid that David was his only chance, he'd had this conversation with him:

> *'Don't worry about a thing,' David told Saul. 'I'll go fight this Philistine!'*
>
> *'Don't be ridiculous!' Saul replied. 'There is no way you can go against this Philistine. You are only a boy, and he has been in the army since he was a boy!' (1 Sam. 17:32-33)*

So it would be accurate to say that David didn't really carry with him the confidence or the support of those closest to him when he went off to face Goliath. Initially he stepped off into battle wearing the king's armour. King Saul had told David to wear his helmet and armoured coat, and to carry his sword.

David took a couple of steps and saw that it wasn't going to work. That's a great lesson to learn. It's no good going out to conquer giants wearing someone else's armour, or doing things the way the world expects you to. God's plan for you is always more important than what other people think or the way they tell you to act.

Eventually, David set off for the big showdown with Goliath armed with just a shepherd's staff, a sling and five stones that he'd bent down to pick up. More importantly, he set off with his future destiny laid out before him by the Lord.

Let battle commence!

When David began to walk towards Goliath, the Philistine giant must have thought he was imagining things. He sneered and shouted at David, trying to make him look even smaller than he was, and eventually yelled to him that he was going feed his body to the birds and the wild animals. It was then that David uttered the sentences that are vital to our understanding of the spiritual principle at the centre of this chapter:

> *David shouted in reply, 'You come to me with sword, spear, and javelin, but I come to you in the name of the LORD Almighty – the God of the armies of Israel, whom you have defied. Today the LORD will conquer you, and I will kill you and cut off your head. And then I will give the dead bodies of your men to the birds and wild animals, and the whole world will know that there is a God in Israel! And everyone will know that the LORD does not need weapons to rescue his people. It is his battle, not ours. The LORD will give you to us!' (1 Sam. 17:45-47)*

After hearing these brave words Goliath moved closer to David, but David actually ran out to meet Goliath – that's how confident he was. He was ready to face the giant head on. He attacked Goliath with one of the five stones he had collected. It hit Goliath in the forehead and he fell face down on the ground. David rushed over and with Goliath's own sword cut the head off the giant.

I often wonder why David had five stones. Was he saying to himself, 'I don't care if I fail with a few of these, but I'm still going to win?' Was he giving himself room for a few mistakes or setbacks before he finally tasted victory? I guess he was prepared to use all five, but only needed one.

When he cut the head off Goliath, David was showing that this was absolutely finished business; that Goliath the giant would never come back. He did all this publicly so that both the Israelite and the Philistine army would see the results. Once the Philistines realized this, they turned and ran away. David had won a mighty victory that was to be a landmark in his life, and a memorable event in the history of the world!

KEY VERSE

David shouted in reply, 'You come to me with sword, spear, and javelin, but I come to you in the name of the LORD Almighty.' (1 Sam. 17:45)

How can we defeat giants?

What are the lessons that we can learn from David? I've summarized them like this:

- He knew God had given him strength in the past
- He knew the battle belonged to the Lord
- He wasn't discouraged by what people said about him
- He didn't try to win the way people said he should
- He wasn't afraid to stand up for himself
- His confidence wasn't so much in himself but in God
- He stepped out 'in the name of the Lord Almighty' (1 Sam 17:4)

Trusting in the name of the Lord

David recognized a great truth: however difficult or daunting a situation looks you can face it strongly if you do it not with your own strength but in the name of the Lord. In Exodus chapter 3, Moses encounters God in a burning bush and God says this to him:

> *God replied to Moses, 'I AM THE ONE WHO ALWAYS IS. Just tell them, "I AM has sent me to you."' God also said, "Tell them, 'The LORD, the God of your ancestors – the God of Abraham, the God of Isaac, and the God of Jacob – has sent me to you." This will be my name forever; it has always been my name, and it will be used throughout all generations.'* (Ex. 3:14-15)

The name of the Lord is dependable and constant, reminding us of his faithfulness. When we step out in the name of the Lord Almighty it means God is on our side; we are not on our own. We are requesting all the power and the authority of God himself when we call on his name.

The story of King Canute is often told as one of a foolish ruler who tried to make the waves of the sea obey him to show everyone how powerful he was. The truth of the story is a little different. King Canute deliberately sat down in the incoming tide to show that however powerful he was, he could never match the power and the authority of God. King Canute said this before he took to the waves: *'Let all men know how empty and worthless is the power of kings. For there is none worthy of the name but God, whom heaven, earth and sea obey.'*[10] He recognized that the real power lay in the name of the Lord and not any earthly ruler.

The New Testament reminds us of the power and authority that the name of Jesus commands: *'Because of this, God raised him up to the heights of heaven and gave him a name that is above every other name, so that at the name of Jesus every knee will bow, in heaven and on earth and under the earth.' (Phil. 2:9-10)*

Followers of Jesus from New Testament times onwards have been baptizing people, healing people, casting out demons, raising people from the dead and defeating giants – all in the name of Jesus. One day every knee in heaven and on earth will bow down to the name of Jesus; and here's the incredible part: we can call out in the name of Jesus today, and we can rely on his supernatural strength in any situation we get into!

Today's giants

In the face of real difficulties we might feel like we are facing unconquerable giants. People will tell us we can never defeat them, or they'll give us worldly advice to try and help us win. Sometimes we'll feel small, and scared, and defeated. We'll call ourselves 'losers' and begin to think that we'll never know what it's like to defeat a giant.

You might be facing one of these modern day giants:

- Addiction to drugs or alcohol
- Feelings of shame because you've been abused
- Family break up
- Fear of the future
- Rejection from friends or family members
- The loss of a loved one
- Failure in school exams
- Bullying
- Illness

Or you may have your own giant.

You need to know that you can call on the name of the Lord Jesus and that he will give you the strength to get through.

Here's a challenge for you! Get your Bible out and a concordance (this lists all the different words in the Bible and where to find them). Check out all the different references for the words 'strong' or 'strength' and prepare to be amazed at how many Bible promises tell us that God will be our strength in times of weakness. Paul in his letter mentions God's 'mighty power' fifteen times. In the name of Jesus, and with God's mighty power you can defeat that giant.

REASONS I DON'T IGNITE

6. Immaturity

One very real way in which we can show immaturity in our faith is when we believe we can do everything in our own strength. We fail miserably, or at least we miss out on the powerful life that God wants for us when we are really dependent on him. Paul says that we should be: *'Fully mature adults, fully developed within and without, fully alive like Christ. No prolonged infancies among us, please...God wants us to grow up.' (Eph. 4:13-15,* The Message*)*

The world will tell us that a sign of maturity is to be physically and mentally strong, not reliant on anyone else. Yet a sign of Christian maturity is to recognize that we are weak and that in our weakest state the Lord can be our strength.

Young Christians often think they know everything, whereas mature Christians realize that there is still so much they don't know or understand: they have learnt more and more to trust in the LORD for their strength and their wisdom. Again, the Apostle Paul tells us how we can be mature:

> *Fix your attention on God. You'll be changed from the inside out. Readily recognize what he wants from you, and quickly respond to it. Unlike the culture around you, always dragging you down to its level of immaturity, God brings the best out of you, develops well-formed maturity in you. (Rom. 12:2,* The Message*)*

Think you know it all and have got life as a Christian sorted? That's not maturity, that's immaturity. Desperately relying on God and knowing you will only get by with his strength? That's maturity!

David finds strength in the Lord

We have already seen in chapter 3 something of Saul's jealousy of David. But to reiterate: soon after David killed Goliath, Saul became jealous. He even offered David his daughter to marry if he fought more battles against the Philistines. Saul secretly hoped David would be killed. Jonathan, Saul's son, helped David escape from the hands of the king and David ran for his life. Samuel died in his old age, and when we pick up the story again, David is now in exile, living in the land of the Philistines in a town called Ziklag, in order to avoid Saul.

Incredibly, David and his band of loyal followers were ready to fight alongside the Philistine army against Saul's army, but some of the Philistine commanders suspected David might double-cross them and swap allegiances, so he was sent home. This is what happened:

> *Three days later, when David and his men arrived home at their town of Ziklag, they found that the Amalekites had made a raid into the Negev and had burned Ziklag to the ground. They had carried off the women and children and*

everyone else but without killing anyone. When David and his men saw the ruins and realized what had happened to their families, they wept until they could weep no more. David's two wives, Ahinoam of Jezreel and Abigail, the widow of Nabal of Carmel, were among those captured. David was now in serious trouble because his men were very bitter about losing their wives and children, and they began to talk of stoning him. But David found strength in the LORD his God. (1 Sam. 30:1-6)

Can you imagine returning to your home and finding the whole town burnt to the ground and your families kidnapped? To make matters worse for David his followers were ready to kill him because they too had lost their homes and their loved ones. What a terrible situation, but once again David looked to the Lord for support; he found strength in the Lord his God.

The story is told of the townsfolk of Feldkirch in Austria, and what happened to them one Easter Sunday. In the Napoleonic wars the town was about to be attacked by Napoleon's massive army. When the townspeople spotted soldiers on the hills around the town, the town council had to make a quick decision. Should they try to defend themselves or offer a white flag of surrender?

As it was Easter, the people had gathered in the town church and the pastor decided that they should carry on with their service, ringing the bells in celebration as they had intended to do, and trusting the Lord for the rest. He explained that the gathered congregation were only thinking of their own weakness and not God's strength to save them.

So the church bells rang, and the French forces thought it meant that the Austrian army had arrived overnight to defend the town. Soon, Napoleon's army began to move on, and by the end of the Easter service had gone completely.[11]

KEY VERSE
But David found strength in the LORD his God. (1 Sam. 30:6)

No situation too tough for God

Flying instructors sometimes put their pupils through a scary test. They tell the pupil to put the plane into a steep dive as if it is going to plummet straight to the ground. After a few seconds, the pupil realizes that the instructor isn't going to help them and they start to panic before they manage to get the plane under control. When they start complaining to the instructor about being reckless, the instructor simply reminds them that there is no situation that the instructor can't get the plane out of! It's all a question of trusting the instructor.

Life is like that. There is no difficult situation, however bleak, that God can't pull you out of or help you survive in. Trust in him and you'll be OK. When the going gets tough some people turn way from God or even blame him for the trouble. Not David. Even in his darkest times such as the instance mentioned, David knew that God would get him through.

Before doing anything else, David began to pray and seek God's guidance, and the Lord told him that if he went after the Amalekites he would recover everything and everyone that had been taken. David trusted the Lord's word and soon set off with his 600 men. After a long journey and twenty-four hours or more of killing the Amalekites, *'David got back everything the Amalekites had taken, and he rescued his two wives. Nothing was missing: small or great, son or daughter, nor anything else that had been taken. David brought everything back.' (1 Sam. 30:18-19)*

David's reliance on the Lord's strength had saved the day again. In a seemingly desperate situation he had demonstrated once more that total dependence on the Lord's power and strength was the only way to live. The Apostle Paul learnt the very same lesson and expressed it this way:

> *This 'foolish' plan of God is far wiser than the wisest of human plans, and God's weakness is stronger than the greatest of human strength. (1 Cor. 1:25)*

And again:

> *For I can do everything with the help of Christ who gives me the strength I need. (Phil. 4:13)*

Honesty time

Have an honesty moment with God right now. Examine this list and see if you are relying on any of these things before you are relying on God:

- Boyfriend or girlfriend
- Family
- Friends
- Money
- Appearance
- Job
- Mobile phone
- Computer
- Intelligence
- Music
- Alcohol
- Drugs
- Church

Spend some time in prayer. Examine your heart and see if there are any areas of your life that you need to bring before God. Ask him to help you to submit to them and to let him be Lord and king of your life again.

'A final word: Be strong in the Lord's mighty power.' (Eph. 6:10)

7 BE GENEROUS WITH THE GIFTS OF GOD

Imagine the winner of *The Weakest Link* sharing all their prize money with the losing contestants, or the winner of *Who Wants to be a Millionaire?* writing a cheque out for every member of the audience. That would be totally revolutionary. When you win a big prize what you do with it is supposed to be simple and easy – you keep it all for yourself!

Life for David was never simple or easy! He experienced another great victory and his popularity soared with his followers but trouble was just around the corner, and we are going to learn another valuable life lesson from David's encounter with the Amalekites. As we saw briefly at the end of the last chapter, a violent battle ensued in which David managed to regain his wives and everything else that the Amalekites had taken. His troops were overjoyed because David brought everything back:

> *His troops rounded up all the flocks and herds and drove them on ahead. 'These all belong to David as his reward!' they said.(1 Sam. 30:20)*

Greedy and jealous

Yet before too long jealousy and greed raise their ugly heads. Two hundred of David's soldiers had been too exhausted to fight the Amalekites. They had stayed behind in Besor Brook and had been guarding equipment, but the soldiers who had done the fighting were none too keen on their exhausted colleagues receiving any of the rewards of the battle:

But some troublemakers among David's men said, 'They didn't go with us, so they can't have any of the plunder. Give them their wives and children, and tell them to be gone.'

But David said, 'No, my brothers! Don't be selfish with what the LORD has given us. He has kept us safe and helped us defeat the enemy. Do you think anyone will listen to you when you talk like this? We share and share alike – those who go to battle and those who guard the equipment.' From then on David made this a law for all of Israel, and it is still followed. (1 Sam. 30:22-25)

Whose money is it anyway?

Incredibly, David not only managed to avoid a nasty argument and a vicious dispute between his own soldiers, he also established new principles for sharing that were built to last.

Before the battle with the Amalekites, David had shown his generosity and compassion by giving food and water to a starving Egyptian slave whose Amalekite owner had been left for dead, and now he was reminding his own followers that everything they had came from the Lord in the first place. It was important not to be selfish with God-given gifts. David's alternative was simple: generosity.

Alexander the Great was a leader who knew all about generosity. There is a story told that Alexander and his advisers were taking a stroll along a road when they came upon a beggar at the side of the road who asked them for a few coins. The man was poor, filthy and seemingly far too unimportant to be speaking to an Emperor. Yet Alexander the Great threw the beggar a handful of gold coins that were very valuable.

One of Alexander's followers was astonished at this, and politely reminded the Emperor that cheap copper coins would have been enough for the beggar. It is said that Alexander replied, 'Copper coins would have suited his needs, but gold coins suited my giving.'[12]

Good news

If there was one person who was entitled to have taken all the plunder for himself it was David, and he would certainly have been justified in deciding that the exhausted troops didn't deserve any reward. But he was really saying to his men that not even he was permitted to keep all the riches of the Amalekites, or even to withhold it from others. All this discussion happened at a place called Besor Brook, which is very revealing. The name 'Besor' means good news or gospel, and it was here that David demonstrated and explained a vital gospel principle.

KEY VERSE

But David said, 'No, my brothers! Don't be selfish with what the LORD has given us.' (1 Sam. 30:23)

David held firm to the belief that being selfish and self-centred went against all that God desires from his people. The men who followed him into battle thought that because they'd done all the work, they deserved all the reward. Now that's fair enough from a purely human economic perspective, but God's economy works very differently. David referred to them all as 'brothers', as if reminding them that as they are all part of God's family the plunder should be shared equally.

David went further, and reminded them that actually it wasn't their effort or work that obtained the plunder anyway. He was clear that they had been rewarded by the Lord, and not as a result of their own ability. David insisted that those too weak to fight actually did play a role in the victory. They had stayed behind to look after baggage and equipment.

Graciously, but firmly, David was laying down the principle that all we have comes as a gift from God and that none of us can lay claim to being a priority when it comes to enjoying the blessing and the gifts of God. It is much better and spiritually healthy for us not to be greedy with the gifts of God but to give them away generously.

Store it up or give it away?

Experts have discovered fascinating differences between the Sea of Galilee and the Dead Sea. The Dead Sea is so full of rich minerals that all living creatures that might once have been there are completely gone. You can't find a living fish, weed, or insect in the Dead Sea. Yet the Sea of Galilee is full of life. Scientists wondered why there was this difference. Both Seas receive water in from streams and creeks, but they discovered that only the Sea of Galilee has streams running out of it. In other words, it doesn't just receive life-giving water: it gives it away too.

David's commitment to being generous with the gifts of God was to remain consistent throughout his lifetime. Towards the end of his life David was overwhelmed when the people of Israel gave willingly and generously so that the Temple could be built. Leaders gave most generously, and the people followed their example. In response, David bowed down and thanked God with this prayer:

Then David praised the Lord *in the presence of the whole assembly:*

'O Lord*, the God of our ancestor Israel, may you be praised forever and ever! Yours,* Lord*, is the greatness, the power, the glory, the victory, and the majesty. Everything in the heavens and on earth is yours, O* Lord*, and this is your kingdom. We adore you as the one who is over all things.*

> *Riches and honor come from you alone, for you rule over everything. Power and might are in your hand, and it is at your discretion that people are made great and given strength.*
>
> *'O our God, we thank you and praise your glorious name! But who am I, and who are my people, that we could give anything to you? Everything we have has come from you, and we give you only what you have already given us! We are here for only a moment, visitors and strangers in the land as our ancestors were before us. Our days on earth are like a shadow, gone so soon without a trace.*
>
> *'O* LORD *our God, even these materials that we have gathered to build a Temple to honour your holy name come from you! It all belongs to you! I know, my God, that you examine our hearts and rejoice when you find integrity there. You know I have done all this with good motives, and I have watched your people offer their gifts willingly and joyously.' (1 Chr. 29:10-17)*

These are David's last recorded words as his son Solomon took over as king with that prayer ringing in his ears. David's final act was to remind all the gathered people, plus the next king, that everything they had came from God in the first place, that they were only holding it temporarily, and that therefore it should all be used for the glory of God.

The $5 or £5 Challenge

My good mate Carl Brettle and I were once speaking at a Leadership Summit in Colorado Springs for a group of 100 business students from Abilene Christian University in Texas.

One night we decided to offer them a challenge. We read out the Parable of the Talents and then gave each student a $5 note. We asked them to use the money as creatively and generously as possible for the Kingdom of God. They could pool their resources and put their money together or they could work alone. We didn't want any money back, and we trusted them to put it to good use.

A couple of months later we got an email from Mike Winegeart, the professor who was organizing the Leadership Summit. Mike detailed the various ways that the students had used the money, and some of the incredible results. Here are just a few of the ways that the students were generous with the money we gave them. Remember that our thinking was that it was actually God's money in the first place anyway. The money was used to:

- Purchase a Bible for an underprivileged child.
- Organize a homeless lunch.
- Pay rent for a needy family.
- Purchase a Chinese Bible.
- Give a tank of petrol to a man in need.
- Make a gift to a children's advocacy centre.
- Make a donation to Tsunami victims in India.
- Contribute towards a summer camp scholarship fund.
- Make a mission gift to Brazil.
- Give a gift to the church janitor.
- Provide lodging at a Salvation Army hostel for the homeless.
- Give clothes for a needy girl.
- Provide packed lunches for the homeless.
- Purchase sermon CDs at church and distribute them.
- Fund Scripture leaflet handouts.
- Support a mission trip to the Ukraine.
- Make a donation to Compassion International for orphans.

Carl and I were blown away by the variety of projects that the students had come up with, and the amounts of money they eventually donated to some of the above, all starting from just $5. Many bought soft drinks and sold them on for a profit; some organized second-hand clothes sales using the $5 for advertising, and others used the money for food and then made sandwiches to distribute. One girl even contacted me to say that a group of students had worked together and raised over $500.

Why don't you take £5 or $5 out of your purse or wallet right now and decide that you are going to use it for the glory of God. See how much more you can give back to the Lord from that original sum.

If you want, you can let me know how you got on by emailing me: Nigel@igniteme.org

Lessons from India

I want to let you into a secret right now. There has been a gap of a couple of months between me writing the rest of this book and this final chapter now. I've been really busy and the publishers, God bless them, graciously gave me an extra month to complete the book. I'm so pleased that I delayed finishing because in that extra month I visited India on a mission trip and learned so many valuable lessons about being generous with the gifts of God.

I'd been invited to India by a friend called Pastor Prasad to work with him and his family for a while in the city of Rajahmundry in southern India. I very quickly discovered that there aren't many rich Christians in India, and that pastors and church leaders face regular financial hardship. Prasad, his parents, brother and their respective families all live together, pooling their resources to support each other and to extend the gospel of Jesus amongst the rural villages surrounding their city.

When I arrived at their house, Prasad showed me to the brand new bedroom and bathroom they had built just for me. Prasad reasoned that as I would struggle in the heat I needed an air-conditioned room with a fridge, and because I was not used to Indian style toilets and showers I would need a western bath and toilet. I was staggered and very humbled that they would go to all that trouble and considerable cost for me. This proved to be typical of their selfless and sacrificial lifestyle.

Prasad had arranged for me to speak at two days of leadership classes for the village pastors he oversees. He had invited 50 but 173 of them arrived for the classes! Prasad was committed to feeding all the pastors for the two days, but he had budgeted for only the 50. Nevertheless, he somehow found the money and the food and everyone was well-fed for the duration of the classes. We even managed to use some money I'd taken with me from the UK to give all the village pastors some travelling expenses to help them get back home by bus rather than by foot.

During my time in India I spoke in many poor village churches, and often saw Christians giving rice, bread and vegetables into the offering. For many people, this practical gift was all they could afford to give, and for many pastors who were struggling to feed themselves and their own family, this was what they needed.

I also visited a church in a leprosy colony and saw how Pastor Prasad and his family cared for this church. We took with us many packets of food for each of the members and I heard how in the winter they were also given clothes and blankets to help them get through the cold nights.

Ignite, the ministry I work for in the UK, donated a sum of money to help complete the construction of a village church, and one of the reasons for my trip was to prepare the way for my wife to help Prasad and his family build a Christian school to serve the village communities.

I very quickly realized that a comparatively small sum of money in western terms will make an immense difference in India. For example, pastors can live on about £30 ($50) a month. I'm committed to partner with Prasad and all his fellow pastors and to help them financially over the next few years.

The great preacher John Wesley was once touring the countryside and he preached a sermon about money to a bunch of farmers. Wesley's first point was 'Get all you can.'

'That's good,' whispered one farmer to another. Wesley's second point was 'Save all you can.' 'Even better,' whispered the farmer. Wesley's third and final point was 'Give all you can.' 'Now he's gone and spoiled it all,' groaned the farmer.[13]

Paul's pattern

So there are many ways that we can be generous with the gifts God has given us if only we'll be selfless enough to make a start.

Just before I left for India my colleague Gary Smith was involved in two concerts: one in Belfast and one in London with the singer Michael W. Smith. Gary was helping raise the profile of the child sponsorship agency Compassion, and over 500 people between the two concerts agreed to sponsor a child through Compassion's worldwide programme.

All of us in the Ignite office sponsor children through Compassion, and we even sponsor two children collectively together in the name of Ignite. This is just one example of the way in which we can help to make a difference.

The Apostle Paul very quickly adopted this sacrificial lifestyle and summed it up in one of his letters to the church in Corinth:

> *So I thought I should send these brothers ahead of me to make sure the gift you promised is ready. But I want it to be a willing gift, not one given under pressure. Remember this*

– a farmer who plants only a few seeds will get a small crop. But the one who plants generously will get a generous crop. You must each make up your own mind as to how much you should give. Don't give reluctantly or in response to pressure. For God loves the person who gives cheerfully. And God will generously provide all you need. Then you will always have everything you need and plenty left over to share with others.

As the Scriptures say,
'Godly people give generously to the poor.
Their good deeds will never be forgotten.'

For God is the one who gives seed to the farmer and then bread to eat. In the same way, he will give you many opportunities to do good, and he will produce a great harvest of generosity in you.

Yes, you will be enriched so that you can give even more generously. And when we take your gifts to those who need them, they will break out in thanksgiving to God. So two good things will happen – the needs of the Christians in Jerusalem will be met, and they will joyfully express their thanksgiving to God. You will be glorifying God through your generous gifts. For your generosity to them will prove that you are obedient to the Good News of Christ. (2 Cor. 9:5-13)

When Paul wrote this he was about to journey to Corinth and wanted to make sure that a collection that the church had earlier been committed to was still going to happen. He wanted to see it was done with willing hearts and not done grudgingly.

Paul used this letter to remind the church in Corinth that God rewards those who give generously, willingly and out of a joyful heart. He used the image of harvest time and challenged the readers to judge for themselves whether they were sowing generously or sparingly. Most importantly, he encouraged the Corinthians that by being generous they would be glorifying God.

REASONS I DON'T IGNITE

7. Indifference

Woe to those who live only for today,
indifferent to the fate of others!
Woe to the playboys, the playgirls,
who think life is a party held just for them!
(Amos 6:5, The Message*)*

One of the major reasons for the start of the Ignite initiative was to shake young people out of a complacency and indifference about their faith. We wanted to prevent a generation growing up and hearing these words from the Lord:

'I know all the things you do, that you are neither hot nor cold. I wish you were one or the other! But since you are like lukewarm water, I will spit you out of my mouth! You say, "I am rich. I have everything I want. I don't need a thing!" And you don't realize that you are wretched and miserable and poor and blind and naked...I am the one who corrects.' (Rev. 3:15-17,19)

Indifference to your own poor condition before God – to God's incredible love for you and to the great gifts he has given you – will mean that you become complacent about life. You will be pre-occupied with serving yourself rather than serving God and others. It's a real shame when you see people who have talents and God-given abilities, but who don't use them to their full potential. So my final commendation to you comes from Paul's words to the Hebrews:

Our great desire is that you will keep right on loving others as long as life lasts, in order to make certain that what you hope for will come true. Then you will not become spiritually dull and indifferent. Instead, you will follow the example of those who are going to inherit God's promises because of their faith and patience. (Heb. 6:11-12)

Honesty time

How generous can you be?

Have an honesty moment before the Lord now and reflect upon how generous you really are. Make a list of all the gifts you believe God has given you and decide how you can be generous with them every day. Your list might include:

- Money
- Clothes
- Food
- Home
- Car
- Friends
- Family
- Time
- Talents and abilities, e.g. playing an instrument
- CDs and DVDs
- Computer
- Mobile phone

You might be able to add some more gifts to the list.

How will you be generous with these each day? Spend some time thinking about how you can make a few simple adjustments to your lifestyle.

RESOURCES

The IGNITE discipleship declaration that is featured throughout this book is an initiative of the Cardiff-based ministry Big Ideas. At the last count, just over 4,000 young people had signed the Ignite declaration. You can do so online at www.igniteme.org for free. If you would like the declaration on a laminated card as most young people do, then this will cost £2, including postage.

Youth leader resources are available to churches and youth leaders who want to encourage young people in their locality to take seriously the challenge of living as a disciple of Jesus. Our website has pages specifically for youth leaders.

The Ignite Leadership Academy is a training programme open to 16-22 year olds and offers a one-night-a-week course for 12 weeks, and involves a residential weekend away. It is designed to produce inspirational leaders for the local church.

The Ignite Cymru Schools Team is a 12 month internship programme that delivers RE lessons and assemblies into high schools all over Wales.

Ignition is a prayer evangelism project aimed to challenge young people and youth groups to pray for their not-yet-Christian friends and to share Jesus with them.

Ignite internships offer young people the opportunity of a gap year as part of the everyday life of the Ignite ministry team.

Ignite Expeditions are short term mission trips overseas, which focus on evangelism amongst young people.

Bible Bits to Ignite your Life is a series of Bible reading notes written for young people and published by Scripture Union.

Big Ideas continue to use contemporary Christian music as a means of evangelism and discipleship. In recent years they have worked in the UK and Europe with Third Day, Rebecca St. James, Newsboys, Michael W. Smith, Skillet, Kathy Burton, Superhero, Eli, Chris Eaton, The Tribe and many more.

For further information on all of the above please visit www.igniteme.org or contact

Ignite
PO Box 39
Dinas Powys,
South Wales
CF64 4ZX
02920 512247
info@igniteme.org

To contact Nigel James directly: nigel@igniteme.org

Endnotes

[1] http://www.britains-smallwars.com/Falklands/vc.htm

[2] This is a paraphrase of the story found on http://www.sermoncentral.com/illustration_topic_results.asp?TopicName=Friend

[3] From *The Complete Book of the Olympics* by David Wallechinsky, quoted on http://www.Sermonillustrations.com/a-z/o/obedience.htm

[4] See http://www.sermonillustrations.com/a-z/o/obedience.htm

[5] Peter Kennedy, Devotional E-Mail, *Devotions in Job*. Copyright permission given. Found on http://www.sermonillustrator.org

[6] Kenneth L. Barker and John R. Kohlenberger III (eds.) *Zondervan* NIV *Bible Commentary* (Grand Rapids: Zondervan, 1994)

[7] Steve Redgrave and Nick Townsend, *A Golden Age* (London: BBC Books, 2001) pp31-32.

[8] This is a paraphrase of the story found on http://www.sermonillustrations.com/a-z/d/dream.htm

[9] See for example Colossians 3:12. The KJV also refers to 'bowels of compassion' in 1 John 3:17.

[10] See http://www.viking.no/e/people/e-knud.htm

[11] Anon.

[12] A paraphrase of the story told on http://www.sermonillustrations.com/a-z/g/generosity.htm

[13] http://www.sermoncentral.com/illustration_topic_results.asp?TopicName=Money&category_name=Stories&topic_id=63

Ignite: God's Purpose for this Generation

by Nigel James

The IGNITE discipleship declaration has been signed by thousands of young people.

By signing this you promise to:

Include Jesus in your moral life, your thoughts, words, actions and relationships.
Grow closer to Jesus through studying the bible, praying and allowing the Holy Spirit to lead you each day.
Network with other Christians .in your city, country and throughout the world.
Involve yourself in a local church and respect its leadership.
Take the message of Jesus into the world by praying, living and witnessing so that everyone may have an opportunity to know Jesus.
Explore God's will for your life and seek to follow it.

Nigel James unpacks and expands the declaration using a combination of personal testimony, biblical teaching and young people's stories. Ready to be passionately committed to Christ? Then read this book.

Revised and updated.

"Ignite – another great idea – may it truly strike a light for a time such as this."
J John, The Philo Trust

"I strongly believe in the essence of Ignite. We all need reminders like the Ignite declaration to spur us on."
Rebecca St. James

ISBN: 1-85078-604-6

Available on www.authenticmedia.co.uk or from your local Christian bookshop

Seven Ways to Ignite an Outrageous Prayer Life

by Nigel James and Carl Brettle

Outrageous prayer is not a new concept or style of praying. It comes straight from the very core of Scripture and is all about having the right heart attitude – an attitude that opens up our lives so that God can intervene in difficult or impossible situations.

Nigel James and Carl Brettle look at the lives of David, Moses, Paul and Hannah and provide seven ways to ignite an outrageous prayer life in you – whether you are a teenager, young adult or youth leader. If you are willing to say 'Lord, teach me to pray' then this book is for you!

Each chapter includes:
- Real life illustrations
- Biblical examples
- Easy to handle teaching
- A novice's guide to key words
- Suggested further reading
- A short prayer to finish

'When we shared the principles of "praying outrageously" in Third Day we really saw God move. Over a period of 2 weeks we began to pray for each of us in the band with a depth and an intensity we hadn't often seen in our ten years together...The idea of praying outrageously is a biblical one and we love it!'
Mac Powell, Third Day

'I strongly believe in the essence of Ignite.'
Rebecca St. James

With a foreword from Phil Togwell of 24-7 Prayer

Nigel James is director of Big Ideas and co-instigator of the IGNITE discipleship initiative. He travels extensively as a speaker and pastor. Carl Brettle played a major role in the 'ten million hours of prayer for Wales' campaign involving people in fifty countries. He works with several strategic prayer organisations.

ISBN: 1-85078-648-8

Seven Myths of Youth Ministry

by Nigel James and Gary Smith

'I commend Nigel and Gary to you and I commend their book. If you've got an ounce of "Factor X" in youth work, *Seven Myths of Youth Ministry* will help you use it effectively.'
Rob Parsons, from the foreword

Seven myths have grown up around ministry to young people and they are dampening the passion needed to excel in youth ministry. Using a combination of biblical truth, real-life examples and comments from a variety of youth leaders themselves, Nigel James identifies these seven myths. He explains why they can be damaging, and points the way to the correct thinking on each issue.

Myths melted are:
- You can really make a difference in your one hour a week
- Size isn't important
- We don't preach, we just sow seeds
- You have to ask them what they want
- Young people lack commitment
- Young people are the future of the church
- We're not in the entertainment business

Not everyone will have been taken in by all the myths, but no-one will be immune. The melting of these myths will help to think through what you are actually doing as a leader. Passionate about youth ministry? You will be after reading this.

"I don't believe there's anything more important we could give ourselves to than raising up radical disciples for Jesus. That's why I'm so delighted that Big Ideas are attempting to do this through their brilliant new Ignite resources."
Andy Hawthorne, Director of The Message Trust

"May the Lord prosper you! There is an enormous need for training in discipleship. Equally, there is an enormous leakage of young people from the churches. You are taking trouble over both. Wonderful."
Rev. Michael Green

ISBN: 1-85078-574-0